The Use of Classical
Spiritual Disciplines
in Evangelical Devotional Life

The Use of Classical
Spiritual Disciplines
in Evangelical Devotional Life

Daniel D. Green

WIPF & STOCK · Eugene, Oregon

THE USE OF CLASSICAL SPIRITUAL DISCIPLINES IN EVANGELICAL
DEVOTIONAL LIFE

ISBN 13: 978-1-55635-531-8

Manufactured in the U.S.A.

*This project is gratefully dedicated
to Betsy for her partnership
in life and ministry*

Contents

Submitted to the Faculty
in partial fulfillment of the requirements
for the degree of
Doctor of Ministry
at Trinity Evangelical Divinity School

Deerfield, Illinois
June 1994

Abstract

THE CLASSICAL spiritual disciplines are so named for their enduring useful-ness to the church. They may be used with success as a means of effect-ing Christian maturity and cultivating heartfelt devotion to God. Among the practices highlighted here are: (1) solitude, (2) journaling, (3) silence, (4) fasting, (5) Bible intake,(6) devotional Bible study, (7) the use of imagination in Bible study, (8) simplicity, (9) practicing the presence,(10) confession (vertical and horizontal), (11) personal and intercessory prayer, and (12) celebration. Also included is an introduction to spiritual disciplines.

Following introductory matter, chapter two offers a theological con-text for the disciplines, before discussing potential benefits and potential dangers of such practices. The theological context asserts that God is know-able, that he initiates contact with his children, and that they are to eagerly respond to his overtures. Potential spiritual benefits covered include spiri-tuality of the heart, production of spiritual fruit, variety for the devotional life, a directed approach to spiritual growth, psychological health, and im-proved corporate worship. Among potential spiritual dangers treated are subjectivity, convergence with unorthodox movements, legalism, pride, and privatization. The project narrative reviews the fourteen class presen-tations. Each discipline is defined, supported scripturally, and commented on by spiritual authorities. Practical tips and assignments accompany each session. An analysis of each lesson, its strengths and weaknesses, is given.

The last chapter of the main body of the project provides an evalua-tion. It is based on various written instruments administered to students. It contains not only evaluation of my teaching effectiveness, but also reports on the student benefits of the project. The latter aspect investigates the im-pact of the disciplines on both depth of relationship with God and general satisfaction with life.

An appendix provides short reviews on 124 important books and articles related to the field. These include general works on spirituality, vol-umes that present several disciplines under one cover, and contributions that focus on a single devotional practice.

1

The Project Introduction

INTIMACY WITH Jesus Christ is an indispensable part of the Christian life. Heartfelt love and devotion toward the Savior are of paramount importance. However, while such intimacy is needed, it is too often lacking.

One reason for this deficiency is that Christians have tended to emphasize objective aspects of the faith, to the neglect of subjective elements. Lovelace expressed this neglect as follows:

> I woke up to the fact that spirituality was a drastically neglected subject among scholars. Christian experience was treated as an optional dimension of spiritual life, a sort of flavor additive that had its place in personal devotion and pastoral work but was marginal as a subject of serious reflection. Scholars focused on the outward shell of the Church's theology and structures but overlooked the vital force that helped make the shell and determine its forms. (Lovelace 1988, 25)

Another explanation, for lack of personal intimacy with Christ, is lack of knowledge. Most believers have not been thoroughly instructed as to how they might go about developing this desired closeness.

Spirituality can be taught. In cooperation with the Holy Spirit, believers can lead fellow-Christians into intimate relationships with the Lord Jesus Christ (Hestenes 1988, 13–20).

The Need for the Project

As the spiritual development of my congregation is one of my main ministry goals, I sense the need to teach them more about how to develop a fervent love for God. I want them to know, specifically, how they can seek a greater closeness with their creator. It is here that classical spiritual disciplines may be employed. They are time-tested means of cultivating fellowship with God. I take to heart Dallas Willard's exhortation:

> At this point in history, every leader among those who identify with Christ as Lord must ask himself or herself: "How can I justify not leading my people into the practice of disciplines for the spiritual life

that would enable them to reign in their lives by Christ Jesus? How can I fail to give them this opportunity?" (Willard 1988, 246)

With primary focus on teaching believers specific ways to develop intimacy with God, I have entitled my project, "The use of classical Spiritual Disciplines in Evangelical Devotional Life."

Primary Objectives

There are three primary objectives to this project: (1) that I will train a group of believers to enhance their spiritual lives through exposure to, and the practice of, a variety of spiritual disciplines, (2) that I will discover how to teach spiritual disciplines more effectively through verbal and written interaction with the group, (3) that I will enhance my own spiritual life through exposure to the literature concerning, and practice of, spiritual disciplines.

Methodology

To carry out this project I will need to conduct selective research from the vast array of literature on the subject. This will include consideration of pertinent books, articles, tapes, and unpublished materials.

Second, I will write two chapters that will be foundational for the teaching of the materials. One will consider theological issues pertaining to the disciplines, and the other will concern selected literature of the disciplines.

Third, I will teach a fourteen week course to a group of laymen meeting in a home study setting. Topics for the sessions include: (1) introduction to spirituality, spiritual disciplines, and course procedures, (2) solitude, (3) journaling, (4) silence, (5) fasting, (6) Bible intake, (7) devotional Bible study, (8) the use of imagination in Bible study, (9) simplicity, (10) practicing the presence, (11) confession (vertical and horizontal), (12) personal and intercessory prayer, (13) celebration, and (14) final summary and sharing.

The project has been approved by the elders of the church. A home has been secured in which to hold the study. It will run from February 18, 1993, through May 20, 1993. Many individuals have been challenged to participate and fifteen have given firm commitments.

Limitations

Several limitations will be placed on this project to make it manageable.

The number of disciplines considered will be twelve. These will provide the group with good variety without becoming unrealistically burdensome.

The participants will be asked to practice the disciplines for 30 minutes, four times a week, for eighteen weeks. The latter will encompass the fourteen weeks of the home study, plus four weeks following it.

Ideally, between fifteen and twenty people will participate. Less than twelve could lessen congregational impact, while more than twenty might negatively impact group dynamics, and complicate evaluation.

Sources

The sources for this project are found in the reference list. Since so much material exists in this subject area, it is desirable to spend the most time with the best sources. Unpublished bibliographies by Rick Cornish, Bruce Demarest, David Larsen, and Carl Lundquist have provided help in locating these.

Evaluation

Three major means will be used to evaluate the project.

Written evaluation will come from three instruments to be filled out by participants. Ellison's "Spiritual Well-Being Scale" will be used in an attempt to bring some objectivity to the process. It will be administered three times during the project, during the first, ninth, and eighteenth weeks, respectively. I will not claim statistical validity for my analysis as this is beyond the scope of my D.Min. program. I will, however, make general observations. A second written form will be "A Spiritual Disciplines Personal Experience Record," which will provide detailed accounts of participant's experiences as they practice the disciplines. My effectiveness as a teacher will be evaluated as class members fill out a modified form of the instrument used by Moody Bible Institute, Chicago, Illinois, to assess teacher capability.

Interaction during class sessions will be the second major means of evaluation. This will allow me to trace progress and make corrections that may be necessitated.

A third means of evaluation will be personal reflection on my methods, and on the spiritual growth of the people in the group.

Anticipation

I look forward, with great excitement, to the project at hand. I foresee significant spiritual benefits for those in my congregation who practice the spiritual disciplines, and expect good for my own life of teaching and devotion.

2

Potential Benefits and Potential Dangers of the Spiritual Disciplines

THIS CHAPTER presents the spiritual disciplines from the standpoint of potential spiritual benefits associated with their proper use, and potential spiritual dangers associated with their improper use. It also provides a brief theological context from which to begin.

Theological Context

This section of the chapter provides a theological context out of which to appreciate the potential benefits and potential dangers of the spiritual disciplines. It deals with God as knowable, God as initiator, and man as respondent.

God as Knowable

The essence of meaningful life, both now and forever, is for man to know his creator, the heavenly Father. Jesus said as much in his high priestly prayer (John 17:3). His statement makes it clear that God the Father can be known personally, as can his son, Jesus Christ.

Jeremiah the prophet teaches us that, above all else, we should revel in the personal knowledge of God. It is to be valued above wisdom, strength, and riches. Knowledge and understanding of God are attainable through the recognition and experience of his attributes (Jer 9:23–24).

God knows each man fully. It may also be said that the believer will one day know God more fully than the constraints of the present life allow (1 Cor 13:12–13).

So then, God is knowable, and the knowledge of God, however imperfect in this life, is of infinite value.

God as Initiator

Not only is God knowable, but he condescends to initiate relationships with humanity. He seeks people to share with spiritually (John 4:23–24).

Such seeking of man is evident as early as Genesis 3:9 in the plaintive cry, "Adam, where are you"? The true God desires to initiate, maintain, and restore intimacy.

Jesus Christ, the Second Person of the Trinity, humbled himself in the kenosis, becoming "God with us" (Matt 1:23). He pitched his tent among men and lived with them (John 1:14). He chose twelve men to be with him as intimate associates in ministry (Mark 3:14). As the light of the world he invited people to follow him and to thus walk in the light of his revelation (John 8:12). Through his death on the cross he removed enmity, and brought reconciliation between God, and those who would place their trust in him (Rom 5:10–11).

God clearly desires human fellowship and offers his to those who will reciprocate.

Man as Respondent

God expects those who claim a personal relationship with him to seek him out. He desires for them to know him personally rather than being caught in externalism (Hos 6:6).

A believer's seeking of God is to be on a spiritual plane and is to be grounded in objective truth (John 4:24). Obedience to this truth, God's Word, will result in a greater self–revelation of God to his followers (John 14:21).

A person is also to seek God in prayer. God invites believers to come boldly to him to have needs met (Heb 4:16) and to see him work on their behalf in extraordinary ways (Jer 33:3). He is also told that persistence will bring answers (Luke 11:9–10).

The apostle Paul was exemplary, laying aside his accomplishments and claim to fame, for the goal of knowing Christ and his power (Phil 3:10).

Perhaps the ideal relationship between man and God is caught in the words of Ps 27:8: "When thou didst say, 'Seek My face,' my heart said to Thee, 'Thy face, O Lord, I shall seek.'"

Summary

God is knowable and, wonderfully, extends himself toward man, offering him a personal relationship. Man is to respond with fervent desire. The means of doing so have been touched upon. Two spiritual disciplines, Bible study, and prayer, have been shown to be effective in relating to God. The next section will show that these disciplines, and others, are key to a rich relationship with God, with all its benefits.

Potential Spiritual Benefits

There are a number of potential spiritual benefits associated with the practice of classical spiritual disciplines. Among these are spirituality of the heart, production of spiritual fruit, variety for the devotional life, a directed approach to spiritual growth, psychological health, and improved corporate worship.

Spirituality of the Heart

Believers in Jesus Christ are commanded to love God not only with their minds, but with their hearts as well (Matt 22:37). Disciples encountering the risen Christ on the road to Emmaus remarked that their hearts burned within them as he explained Scripture (Luke 24:32).

Yet such a response is not automatic. In fact, it is often missing, even among those who most revere the Word of God. Benner (1988, 96) is right in stating: "Evangelicalism's rationalistic approach to theology, and activistic approach to the Christian life have often tended to make it quite shallow. Morton Kelsey has observed: "In Protestantism, God became a theological idea known by inference, rather than a reality known by experience" (Kelsey 1982, 11). Tozer bemoans such cold orthodoxy:

> There is today no lack of Bible teachers to set forth correctly the principles of the doctrines of Christ, but too many of these seem satisfied to teach the fundamentals of the faith year after year, strangely unaware that there is no manifest Presence or anything unusual in their personal lives. They minister constantly to believers who feel within their breasts a longing which their teaching simply does not satisfy. (Tozer 1982, 9)

Demarest and Raup summarize the problem and the need:

> Persons created in the image of God are not adequately nourished by a faith that is primarily intellectual or moralistic. For example,

the mere thought of food will not satisfy a hungry person. Nothing short of actual food will suffice. So it is that Christians hunger and thirst for participation in God that strikes a chord of reality in their total lived experience. Believers need personally to discover and relate to the God who not only engages their minds, but who lovingly reveals Himself to their hearts. (Demarest and Raup 1989, 322–323)

If those with a keen desire for orthodoxy will also pursue classical disciplines, a wedding of mind and heart, for God, can occur.

John Wesley was deeply influenced by classics of spirituality written by William Law, Francis de Sales, and Thomas à Kempis. These, along with family training, apparently led Wesley into such practices as Bible study, prayer, fasting, sharing, and singing. The result was a Methodism historic in its fervency (Benner 1988, 97).

Bloesch, in advocating such disciplines as prayer, fasting, meditation, simplicity, hymn-singing, and silence, says:

If anything characterizes modern Protestantism, it is the absence of spiritual disciplines or spiritual exercises. Yet such disciplines form the core of the life of devotion. (Bloesch 1988a, 49)

Lawrence O. Richards affirms that growth in experiential intimacy is stimulated by such practices as solitude, prayer of the heart, meditation, and practicing the presence (Richards 1987, 106–108).

Demarest and Raup urge quiet and reverent listening, and thoughtful repetition of scriptural phrases, as ways of developing intimacy, and conclude:

By advancing these proposals we do not advocate the formation of another (evangelical) renewal movement. We do, however, urge a renewal of the biblical practice of heart-intimacy with God by encouraging evangelical Christians to utilize time-honored and edifying spiritual disciplines. . . . By so recovering authentic Christian spirituality the believer will joyfully discover that head, hands, and heart unite as a powerful force for God in a dry and thirsty land. (Demarest and Raup 1989, 325–326)

Production of Spiritual Fruit

Galatians 5:22–23 lists the fruit of the Spirit as love, joy, peace, patience, kindness, goodness, faithfulness, gentleness, and self-control. When these are present they evidence spiritual maturity. This section will show a strong relationship between the practice of spiritual disciplines and the presence of these characteristics.

Solitude and silence have been instrumental in production of spiritual fruit. Dirk Nelson testifies of the peace, patience, and joy that are the result of these disciplines:

> The more I practice this discipline, the more I appreciate the strength of silence. The less I become skeptical and judgmental, the more I learn to accept the things I didn't like about others, the more I accept them as uniquely created in the image of God. The less I talk, the fuller are words spoken at an appropriate time. The more I value others, the more I serve them in small ways, the more I enjoy and celebrate my life. The more I celebrate, the more I realize that God has been giving me wonderful things in my life, the less I worry about my future. I will accept and enjoy what God is continuously giving to me. I think I am beginning to really enjoy God. (Willard 1988, 165)

Solitude, combined with an extended fast, helped produce unparalleled faithfulness in the Lord Jesus, as He withstood Satan's onslaught in the wilderness (Luke 4:1–15).

Fasting has often been linked to increased self control. Willard says: "Fasting teaches temperance or self control and therefore teaches moderation and restraint with regard to all our natural drives" (Willard 1988, 167). Others have experienced increased peace through the discipline. One writer attested that, when he had established the practice, "a new peace, unknown before, settled over my life" (Anderson 1977, 112).

Study of the Bible is associated with great joy (Ps 119:62, Jer 15:16), self-control (Ps 119:9), faithfulness (Luke 4:4–12), and love (1 Pet 1:22–23).

Simplicity leads logically to peace, in the form of diminished anxiety (Luke 12:22–34). In bringing peace it also frees the believer to pursue faith, love, and gentleness (1 Tim 6:6–11). Joy may also result. As one author says: "The inward reality of simplicity involves a life of joyful unconcern for possessions" (Foster 1978, 87).

Prayer, in its various forms, also results in spiritual fruit. Petition is related closely to joy (John 16:24) and petition, with thanksgiving, to supernatural peace (Phil 4:6–7). Confession relieves emotional and physical stress, and restores joy, faithfulness, and peace (Pss 32:1–7, 51:7–17). Practicing the presence, the staying of the mind on God, also bears with it the promise of complete peace (Isa 26:3).

Variety for the Devotional Life

The decline of devotional life is sometimes related to boredom with routine. Typically, Evangelicals concentrate on devotional Bible study and petitionary prayer, neglecting the many other forms that devotion can take. Several spiritual disciplines are commanded in Scripture. Among these are Bible study (2 Tim 2:15), meditation (Josh 1:8), petition (John 16:24), confession (1 John 1:9), and intercession (Jas 5:16). Others are implied, such as solitude (Matt 14:23), silence (Ps 46:10, Hab 2:20), secrecy (Matt 6:18), fasting (Matt 9:14–15), practicing the presence (1 Thess 5:17), and simplicity (1 Tim 6:7–8). Still others, such as journaling and devotional reading, are not mentioned in Scripture, but are often helpful. It is not necessary for dryness to set in due to a limited range of practices being employed. When multiple disciplines are used, spiritual freshness may be maintained more easily.

Variety of disciplines may also be indicated by personal needs at particular times of year, or stages of life. Thomas à Kempis states:

> All cannot have one exercise, but one suiteth better to this man, and one to that. Even for the diversity of season different exercises are needed, some suit better for feasts, some for fasts. We need one kind in time of temptations and others in time of peace and quietness. Some are suitable for our times of sadness, and others when we are joyful in the Lord. (Kempis 1984, 1:19:2)

Bloesch concurs:

> Spiritual exercises must be voluntarily undertaken, and they must be abandoned once they have outlived their usefulness. Just as athletes need to proceed from one exercise to another in order to excel in their particular field, so Christians need to practice a variety of spiritual exercises if they are to run the race of life successfully. (Bloesch 1988a, 59)

Varying disciplines also promotes balance in the devotional life. Willard (1988, 158) urges believers to maintain equilibrium by matching disciplines of abstinence (solitude, silence, fasting, frugality, chastity, secrecy, and sacrifice) with those of engagement (study, worship, celebration, service, prayer, fellowship, confession, and submission). Thus, devotional practice touches both the public and private sphere of life. He concludes:

> Practicing a range of activities that have proven track records across the centuries will keep us from erring. And if, later, other activities

are really more what we need, our progress won't seriously be hindered, and we'll probably be led into them. (Willard 1988, 158)

A Directed Approach to Spiritual Growth

Many believers lack adequate guidance in the pursuit of spiritual growth. They do not know how to go about it, nor how to sustain it once they start. The need is for direction and discipline. The disciple is commanded to discipline himself toward the goal of godliness (1 Tim 4:7), and to pursue holiness (Heb 12:14), with the assurance that God has given him the capacity to exercise such obedience (2 Tim 1:7).

A number of writers have been insistent that the spiritual disciplines are the instruments through which discipline unto godliness is to be exercised.

Richard Foster says of the classical disciplines:

> They are God's means of grace. The inner righteousness we seek is not something that is poured on our heads. God has ordained the Disciplines of the spiritual life as the means by which we place ourselves where he can bless us. . . . The grace of God is unearned and unearnable, but if we ever expect to grow in grace we must pay the price of a consciously chosen course of action which involves both individual and group life. Spiritual growth is the purpose of the disciplines. (Foster 1978, 7–8)

Donald Whitney introduces his book on a similar note:

> I will maintain that the only road to Christian maturity and godliness (a biblical term synonymous with Christlikeness and holiness) passes through the practice of the Spiritual Disciplines. I will emphasize that Godliness is the goal of the Disciplines, and when we remember this, the spiritual Disciplines become a delight instead of drudgery. . . . The Spiritual disciplines are the God-given means we are to use in the Spirit-filled pursuit of Godliness. . . . God has given us the Spiritual Disciplines as a means of receiving His grace and growing in Godliness. By them we place ourselves before God for Him to work in us. (Whitney 1991, 14–15)

Kempis, in urging determined use of the disciplines, says:

> According to our resolution so is the rate of our progress, and much diligence is needful for him who would make good progress. . . . But manifold causes bring about abandonment of our resolution, yet a trivial omission of holy exercises can hardly be made without some loss to us. (Kempis 1984, 1:19:2)

The believer who is willing to practice classical disciplines will not find his spiritual life without direction. Practiced under the influence of the Holy Spirit, they will guide him toward maturity.

Psychological Health

Psychological problems are epidemic in the modern world. People are unable to adequately deal with the pressures of life. In summarizing a number of studies, Frank Minirith says:

> Twenty billion dollars are spent annually coping with the widespread mental problems afflicting out country. . . . Moreover, approximately one million pounds of barbiturates are manufactured annually. Also, patients suffering from mental problems crowd into our hospitals at the rate of three for every ten patients admitted, and the tenth leading cause of deaths bears the grim label, SUICIDE. . . . Another study revealed that 80 percent of the population had significant psychiatric symptoms. . . . These data indicate a heartrending affirmation that people are earnestly in need of guidance and counsel. (Minrith 1977, 19)

Unfortunately these problems are not escaped by a host of Christians, who are rushing to psychotherapists with their unmet needs (Demarest and Raup, 323). Christians have reason to believe that the answer for many psychological problems is strongly related to a healthy spiritual life. The promises of God's Word are said to bring hope (Ps 119:49). Physical and psychological problems sometimes come from sin (Ps 38:3–4, 18), their cure from confession (Ps 32:3–5). Indeed, the spiritual and psychological aspects of the believer cannot be separated. As Laidlaw has observed:

> Human individuality is of one piece, it is not composed of separate or independent parts. The assertion is essential to the theology of the whole Bible. (Benner 188, 110)

Lovelace agrees, and goes on to suggest that the treatment of psychological problems ought to be spiritual:

> On the other hand, we cannot isolate "spiritual" problems for "psychological" problems and treat the latter nonspiritually because the human soul is a psychospiritual continuum in which psychological stress, physiological conditions and spiritual states are deeply interrelated. (Lovelace 1979, 220)

Clinical psychologist David Benner believes that spiritual and psychological maturity should coincide:

> The norm . . . is that spiritual growth should lead to psychological growth. People who appear to be spiritual giants but are actually psychological cripples may not be all they appear to be spiritually. (Benner 1988, 126)

It has been shown above that classical spiritual disciplines play a part in producing spiritual fruit. Among this fruit are joy, peace, patience, and self control, all important components in mental health. It should not be surprising, then, to find that researchers, clinicians, and spiritual leaders do link the practice of classic disciplines to psychological recovery and health.

One study found that some forms of prayer impact mental health in significant ways. Meditative prayer (sometimes called contemplation, or practicing the presence) was found to positively impact experiential well-being. Colloquial prayer (the mixing of thanksgiving, praise, and adoration) was a factor in personal happiness (Poloma and Pendleton 1981, 71–81).

Bowman links confession with the easing of anxiety related to guilt, saying:

> No way of escape from guilt is found for the sufferer except through a functioning confession. Certain psychological and spiritual dynamics are involved which make it necessary that this need to confess be directed toward a lifting of the guilt. (Bowman 1969, 30)

John Morgan promotes silence as creative therapy, urging pastors to talk less, thus entering listening quiet with their counselees. He even finds silence helpful in the healing of the mentally ill (Morgan 1975, 248–251).

Several studies suggest a positive effect of fasting on mental function, and overall psychological health (Akakios 1989, 91–92).

Minirth, Meier, Hawkins, and Flournoy illustrate the point:

> Often, when one feels the pressure of burnout, the first thing to be eliminated is the time for personal reflection, meditation, and spiritual devotion. The pressures of a busy schedule, coupled with an increasing inability to keep up, crowd out a time for meditating on the Word, which is essential in keeping a sharp edge spiritually, mentally, and physically. (Minirth and others 1986, 33–34)

By nurturing the soul, the believer cares for his mind as well.

Improved Corporate Worship

The Christian cannot make the spiritual journey alone He must travel with a family, and engage in meaningful, shared worship. Benner says:

> First, the Christian's relationship with God is not exclusively a personal possession. Christian spirituality is also corporate spirituality. The life of Christ is found in community, and growth in spirituality is similarly found in relationship with the body of Christ, the church. (Benner 1988, 102–103)

But the American church is experiencing a crisis with regard to worship. Services by the hundreds are being overhauled in an effort to bring more meaning to individual lives, and to reach the lost. Yet the adoration of a holy God is too often lacking. Bloesch sees the solution not in liturgical overhaul, but in deepened individual devotion:

> The crisis in personal piety is indubitably related to the crisis in corporate worship. James White, Robert Webber, and others rightly criticize the poverty in the worship services of popular evangelicalism where people come to be entertained rather than to praise God. Yet it is questionable whether the retreat to high-churchism can be the answer to the crisis in piety. (Bloesch 1988a, xii)

The point is that while disciplines of engagement such as fellowship, service, horizontal confession, and submission more obviously enhance worship, disciplines between the individual and God are also foundational. Brother Lawrence, for instance, associated his experience of God in the kitchen with his ability to worship with others at Mass (Foster 1978, 162).

One can reasonably expect that his private seeking and adoration of God will enhance the worship of his local congregation. As one writer puts it:

> Faith and life go together, but being precedes doing. And this means that inward communion with the living Christ made possible by the outpouring of the Holy Spirit is the basis for both church reform and social holiness. (Bloesch 1988a, xiii)

Potential Spiritual Dangers

There are a number of spiritual dangers to be avoided while practicing spiritual disciplines. Among these are subjectivity, convergence with unorthodox movements, legalism, pride, and privatization.

Subjectivity

While the life of devotion should impact the emotional life of the believer, it must find its ground in the objective truths of Scripture.

It is through God's Word that the believer is set aside for his holy purposes (John 17:17). Through it he finds instruction, reproof, correction, instruction in righteousness, and adequacy for good works (2 Tim 3:16–17). It causes him to be born again, and thus deserves his undivided attention (Jas 1:18–19). It is through the power of Scripture that growth occurs (2 Pet 1:4–7).

Some, however, have construed a concept of Christian spirituality that is not sufficiently grounded in the Word. Schleiermacher, for instance, said: "It matters not what conceptions a man adheres to, he can still be pious" (Schleiermacher 1958, 95). Others, legitimately involved in spiritual disciplines, have neglected their foundation. Jacob Boehme favored subjective criteria over revelation, saying:

> Though an angel from heaven should tell this to me, yet for all that I could not believe it, much less lay hold on it; for I should always doubt whether it was certainly so or no. But the Sun itself arises in my spirit, and therefore I am sure of it. (Boehme 1954, 47)

Morton Kelsey, a leader in the disciplines of silence and solitude, places undue authority in dream experience:

> God gives us dreams to help manage our lives and bring us to the other. . . . Dreams give us clues as to how to run our lives. . . . Learning to listen to dreams may well be learning to listen and work actively with God. (Kelsey 1980, 109)

Thomas Kelly, who wrote profoundly on simplicity and practicing the presence, seems to lack objectivity with regard to guidance as shown below:

> Deep within us all there is an amazing inner sanctuary of the soul . . . a speaking voice, to which we may continuously return. . . . Eternity is at our hearts . . . calling us home to Itself. Yielding to these persuasions . . . to the Light Within, is the beginning of true life. (Kelly 1941, 29)

Donald Bloesch issues a warning against such unbalanced mysticism:

> I believe more strongly than before that a theology of Christian commitment must be united with a theology of the Word of God if it is not to lapse into subjectivism. . . . The focus on personal piety must never supplant the more basic focus on the life, death, and resurrection of Jesus Christ. (Bloesch 1988a, xi–xii)

Arthur Johnson, in a critique of mysticism within Evangelical circles, says:

> This belief sees truth and knowledge as attainable through mystical experience. All truth is tested by inner, subjective impressions rather than by its logical consistency or other relational consideration. . . . The resulting view leads the person to equate his inner impressions or subjective states with the voice of God. (Johnson 1988, 26)

Winfried Corduan, in response to Johnson, expresses the difficulty this way:

> The danger in mysticism is not located where Johnson places it. The problem is not whether we come to know truth through experience, but whether the experience and the truth that it points to are wholly subordinate to the Bible. (Corduan 1991, 121)

One need not choose between objectivity and experience in the Christian life. Objective truth should lead to proper feelings. However, feelings must never reign. P. T. Forsyth summarizes the issue well:

> The experimental religion of true faith is not based on experience, but on revelation and faith. It is realized by experience, it proceeds in experience; but it does not proceed from experience. . . . Our faith is not in our experience, but in our Saviour. (Forsyth 1957, 108)

Convergence With Unorthodox Movements

Readings in the area of spirituality and spiritual disciplines can lead the seeker of God unwittingly astray into unorthodox movements. Among these are asceticism, Catholicism, Eastern Mysticism, the New Age Movement, and quietism.

Asceticism

While certain spiritual disciplines such as fasting, simplicity, and solitude are helpful forms of self denial, the consideration here is of the type that departs from the Bible. The asceticism to be avoided is the extreme form that stresses self denial as meritorious in the sight of God (Col 2:20–23, 1 Tim 4:1–5).

Rosemary Rader describes how ascetic practices sometimes acquired a perverted focus in the early church:

> Asceticism became the most effective way of acquiring assurance of salvation. In the struggle for mastery over the temptations of the

world, the flesh, and demonic powers, the soul could make its ascent to God from whom it had fallen by disobedience. (Wakefield 1983, 24)

Salvation is by faith and must never be placed as something earnable through any practice of man.

Nor does God take pleasure in pain. As Wallis observes: "Here lurks that insidious pride which glories in its own readiness to embrace suffering instead of glorying in the cross" (Wallis 1968, 90).

Extreme asceticism has often been a distraction from true spirituality rather than a help to it. As Kelsey notes:

When matter or the body or the human spirit are seen as either valueless or evil, then one has no choice but to beat down these obstacles to the religious way. Whether this view results in wearing hair shirts and spiked chains, in sitting for years on a pillar, or eating only cabbage leaves, or in simply refusing to participate in life as it is in this world, it is equally dangerous. The person glories in asceticism and forgets love. It is all too easy to be heroic about a belief like this and to forget how much heroism it takes to give real love. (Kelsey 1976, 99)

Forms or denial should be seen as potential means of developing intimacy with God, and never as instruments of gaining his approval.

Catholicism

Roman Catholic theologians and practitioners have contributed an enormous volume of work to the fields of spirituality and spiritual disciplines. Ancient writers such as John of the Cross, Teresa of Avila, and Thomas á Kempis wrote valuable works, as have moderns such as Richard Hauser, Morton Kelsey, Thomas Merton, and Henri Nouwen.

One can gain great insight from reading these authors At the same time great caution must be exercised, for they belong to a movement that stands outside of biblical orthodoxy. These writers, consistent with their theological orientation, embrace the doctrines of salvation by faith plus works, the Mass, Mariolatry, and veneration of images. This is not to say that their writings should not be read. It is to say, however, that Evangelicals, and especially novices, should undertake such reading with spiritual guardedness, lest they be swept into serious misemphases.

Eastern Mysticism

Mystical elements are not unique to Christianity. They belong to many religions, especially those from the East. With Eastern thought strongly impacting Western culture, Evangelicals need to be careful not to embrace harmful religious thought and practice.

Anthony de Mello advocates Christian disciplines in Eastern form. While his work is at points beneficial, it also advocates excessive attention to body sensations, breathing techniques, and mind-body dichotomy (de Mello 1978, 15, 37, 96). He also encourages the emptying of the mind for the purpose of communing with God:

> Now that is just what is demanded of some people if they would go deep into communion with the Infinite, with God: gaze for hours at a blank. Some mystics recommend that we gaze at this blank lovingly. And it requires a good deal of faith to gaze with love and yearning at what seems like nothing when we first get in touch with it. (de Mello 1978, 30)

In response to de Mello, Hingley warns:

> If such techniques have any value at all, it must be recognized that it is only a limited one. It is dangerous to confuse them with prayer: at best, they can only be a preparation for prayer. There is therefore a danger in such techniques if they become a substitute for Christian meditation and prayer, rather than preparation for it; and they may also be dangerous for people who have come to Christ out of a background in Yoga or Eastern mysticism, and still feel its attraction. (Hingley 1990, 87)

Thomas Merton, in the guise of open-mindedness and maturity says:

> I need not add that I think I have now reached a stage (long overdue) of religious maturity at which it may be possible for someone to remain perfectly faithful to a Christian and Western monastic commitment, and yet to learn in depth, say, from a Buddhist discipline and experience. . . . I believe that by openness to Buddhism, Hinduism, and these great Asian traditions, we stand a wonderful chance of learning more about the potentiality of our own traditions. . . . The combination of the natural techniques and graces and the other things that have been manifested in Asia, and the Christian liberty of the gospel should bring us all at last to that full and transcendent liberty which is beyond mere cultural differences and mere externals. (Merton 1968, xxiii–xxiv)

Francis Schaeffer, in advancing Christian mysticism over the Eastern variety says:

> One is not asked to deny the reason, the intellect, in true Christian mysticism. And there is to be no loss of personality, no loss of the individual man. In Eastern mysticism—for which the West is searching so madly now that it has lost the sense of history, of content, and the truth of biblical facts—there is always finally the loss of personality. It cannot be otherwise in their framework. . . . This is Eastern mysticism. It is grounded in the loss of personality of the individual. Not so Christian mysticism. Christian mysticism is communion with Christ. It is Christ bringing forth fruit through me, the Christian, with no loss of personality and without my being used as a stick or stone either. (Schaeffer 1971, 54)

Nor can any sort of spirit-body dichotomy be entertained within Christian orthodoxy. God has made both, and pronounced both honorable. Christians believe that: "The spiritual and bodily are by no means opposed in human life—they are complimentary" (Willard 1988, 75). Meister Eckhart said: "No soul can really do anything except through the body to which it is attached" (Blakney 1941, 253). Willard's summary is helpful: "Human personality is not separable in our consciousness from the human body. And that fact is expressed by asserting the IDENTITY of the person as his or her body" (Willard 1988, 84).

Neither mind, soul, or body are disposable, at any time, in Christian life. Nor is an openness to Buddhism and Hinduism admirable. Spiritual writers who think otherwise present a potential danger to those seeking Christ through the disciplines.

The New Age Movement

Closely akin to Eastern religions mentioned above is the New Age Movement. Douglas Groothius says:

> For about two decades Eastern religions have been moving West and aggressively seeking converts among secularists and Christians. Now a kind of ecumenical movement of Eastern, occult and New Consciousness groups network together in the New Age Movement. (Groothuis 1986, 9)

While not advocating New Age tenets directly, some practitioners of the spiritual disciplines lead their followers toward dangerous territory. Morton Kelsey, advocating aids in the use of silence says:

Yoga, which has been used since ancient times in India, is now valued by many Christians. The repetition of a mantra and concentration on a mandela can also be used as ways of turning inward. Some people find the use of an illogical question, which is called a koan in Zen practice, puts one's analytical mind at rest and offers freedom and a new source of insight. (Kelsey 1976, 109)

Some seminaries are now including, with classics such as *The Imitation of Christ* and *The Practice of the Presence of God*, such works as *Mother Earth Spirituality* and *Original Blessing*. In these latter works, says Bloesch:

Affirming Christ as the only way is condemned as a form of ethnocentrism, "arrogant and uncompassionate in a world of pluralism, a world in which there are many worthwhile ways." (Bloesch 1991, 22)

Thus, in a context of classic disciplines, New Age thought is introduced.

Quietism

Some practitioners of contemplation have been understood to embrace quietism. Because contemplation is not as objective and active as scriptural meditation, it has been inferred that it is therefore entirely passive.

Although not totally passive herself Guyon wrote:

All spirituality is reduced to the simple working of God in oneself, and in a complete indifference to everything, even to virtue and one's own salvation, and in complete abandonment to the will of God as regards reprobation and eternal happiness. According to these principles it is no longer necessary to meditate on the great truths of the Gospel or on the mysteries of the life and death of Jesus Christ. (Lawrence 1977, 22)

Simone Weil spoke similarly:

The most beautiful life possible has always seemed to me to be one where everything is determined, either by the pressure of circumstances or by impulses . . . where there is never any room for choice. (Meadow 1984, 113)

This is not to say that all contemplatives have quietist leanings. Far from it. Lawrence Richards, a proponent of contemplation says: "Human beings must accept the responsibility for their own spiritual life and for helping others along the road of spiritual growth" (Richards 1987, 16).

The point is this. Many contemplatives have become passive my misunderstanding and abusing contemplation. Such abuse is a peril to avoid.

Legalism

Legalism may be defined as strict adherence to law or prescription. Those who practice spiritual disciplines need to be wary of a tendency to lose sight of God's grace, and their standing by grace, while pursuing a deeper relationship with God.

The distinction between prescriptive and descriptive disciplines is critical. Prescriptive disciplines are those commanded by Scripture. As mentioned in this chapter's section on variety for the devotional life, they include Bible study, meditation, petition, confession, and intercession. Other disciplines are descriptive. They are only suggested, or implied, ways of deepening a relationship with God, and should not be considered, or taught, as obligations. Among these are journaling, the biblical use of imagination, and simplicity.

Historically, some on the spiritual journey have slipped into the error of demanding descriptive practices.

Bill Faw criticizes his own Brethren movement for excessive emphasis on simplicity:

> We talked about staying away from "everything that is high, without exception . . . , that brethren should not dress, build or decorate houses "in the style of those high in the world". . . . Many specific decisions were made about what members could and could not have in their homes, on their carriages, or on their bodies. Through much of the last century Brethren were not even to have their picture or portrait made because it might lead to pride. (Faw 1984, 152)

William Law went so far as to insist that each period of devotion begin the same way:

> There is one thing still remaining that you must be required to observe not only as fit and proper to be done, but as such as cannot be neglected without great prejudice to your devotions; and that is, to begin all your prayers with a Psalm. This is so right, so beneficial to devotion, has so much effect upon our hearts, that it may be insisted upon as a common rule for all persons. (Law 1966, 163)

Implicit practices need to be recognized as valuable and suggestive, but should not be elevated to the level of commanded disciplines.

Another feature of legalism to be guarded against is externalism. It is the rigid compliance with spiritual practices apart from sincerity. It is also concern for appearance rather than reality. It is warned against in Scripture (Matt 6:1–18, 23:4).

Jerry Falwell says of fasting: "The credibility of fasting is not in abstention from food but in the sincerity of the person who manifests his faith by withholding himself from food" (Falwell 1981, 30).

Richard Foster states:

> It is easy in our zeal for the Spiritual Disciplines to turn them into the external righteousness of the scribes and Pharisees. When the disciplines degenerate into law, they are used to manipulate and control people. (Foster 1988, 10)

Roberta Hestenes comments on the need to respect individual freedom:

> We have to remember that people are on different spiritual journeys and have different needs and circumstances and temperments. Therefore, not everyone should do the same spiritual disciplines in the same ways. We want to respect that God-given diversity. (Hestenes 1988, 16)

Legalism, then, in the practice of spiritual disciplines, may manifest itself in the prescription of descriptive practices, in externalism, and in the wish to control the behavior of other believers.

Pride

Another potential peril of spiritual practices is pride. Pride exults itself, and clamors for attention, because its practitioner is engaged in disciplines.

The Pharisees were found guilty of being proud of their religious practices. They enjoyed the recognition of the Jewish community that was related to their presumed piety (Mark 12:38–39), and flaunted their use of Scripture (Matt 23:5). Others in Jesus' day made a public display of their giving, prayer, and fasting (Matt 6:1–5, 16). The Corinthians apparently felt that they had arrived spiritually (1 Cor 4:7–8).

Morton Kelsey warns against pride as the result of journaling insights:

> The idea that one has special value because one has insights can lead to real trouble. Most often when ordinary people think they have a special connection with divine reality, they are inflated and not very critical. Any special insight should be checked out with the critical evaluation of another so that one does not get into nonsense. I am very suspicious of those who feel themselves above this kind of critical evaluation. (Kelsey 1980, 97)

Thomas á Kempis was wary of pride with regard to the contemplative life and said:

> I love no contemplation that leadeth to pride . . . Willingly do I accept that grace whereby I am made humbler and more wary, and more ready to renounce myself. (Kempis 1984, 2:10:3)

The proper attitude is that God has graciously granted salvation and that he is the primary agent in sanctification. Believers seek to cooperate with God in their spiritual growth through using spiritual disciplines. Nevertheless, the ultimate direction of their spiritual development remains outside our control (Benner 1988, 107). Acknowledging this truth should lead us to humbly conclude with Merton; "We do not want to be beginners. But let us be convinced of the fact that we will never be anything but beginners all our life" (Merton 1969, 37).

Privatization

Privatization has to do, as expressed by Guiness, with the undesirable separation of the believer's private and public lives:

> By privatization I mean the process by which modernization produces a cleavage between public and private spheres of life and focuses the private sphere as the special arena for the expansion of individual freedom and fulfillment. (Guiness 1983, 74)

Many of the classical spiritual disciplines take place in private. But it is not God's will that the believer be cloistered to the extent that he fails to impact the outside world. The Christian is to be salt to the earth (Matt 5:13) and light for the world (Matt 5:14). While the individual devotional life is to be private (Matt 6:1–18), good works should often be public (Matt 5:16). Believers as a whole are to be aggressive in evangelism (Matt 28:16–20) and concerned about the physical needs of all people (Gal 6:9–10). Of the estimate that one quarter of the population of the United States has professed a conversion experience William Iverson says: "A pound of meat should surely be affected by a quarter pound of salt" (Willard 1988, 23).

Thomas á Kempis seems to have fallen into Privatization, urging a separation from fellow-men:

> To him who withdraweth himself from his acquaintance and friends God with his holy angels will draw nigh. . . . It is praiseworthy for a religious man to go seldom abroad, to fly from being seen, to have no desire to see men. (Kempis 1984, 1:20:6)

Henri Nouwen countered this extreme, urging that solitude be seen as a catalyst for social action: "Thus, in and through solitude we do not move away from people. On the contrary, we move closer to them through compassionate ministry" (Nouwen 1981, 24).

Bloesch also sees devotion and action as going hand-in-hand, saying: "Devotion entails piety, that is the fear of God, but it also includes mercy, service to our fellow humanity" (Bloesch 1988a, 16).

This proper connection between devotional life and social responsibility is often realized in American Evangelicalism. Harold O. J. Brown comments on a Gallup poll that demonstrated that regular Bible readers are strongly concerned about ethics and social responsibility:

> From this poll it is possible to draw the conclusion that evangelicals are a highly moral people, more concerned about God and more concerned about the welfare of their fellow human beings than any other group polled. . . . it is evident that continuing Christian discipleship, and particularly serious attention to the Bible and its message on a regular basis, does motivate Christians across the board of personal and social concerns. (Brown 1980, 29)

Nevertheless the danger of an isolated devotional life remains. In the words of Bloesch: "By dividing Christ and culture, the way is opened for an interiorized religion" (Bloesch 1988a, 110).

But the goal of the believer should be to allow a vital devotional life to move him to action in all realms of life. Let the words of Dallas Willard conclude:

> So humankind's job description is clearly stated. We were not designed just to live in mystic communion with our Maker, as so often suggested. Rather, we were created to govern the earth with all its living things. (Willard 1988, 48)

3

The Project Narrative

THE PURPOSE of this chapter is to provide an overview of the project from the inception of the idea, through the presentation of class sessions. It includes an account of preliminary work, a general profile of participants, and a summary of each class session.

Preliminary Work

This idea for this project first came to my mind in the fall of 1990, while preparing for Bruce Demarest's Doctor of Ministry course entitled "Theology and the Spiritual Journey: The Pathway of the Heart." I had struggled to find a topic for my major project that really compelled me. I was also experiencing dissatisfaction in my own spiritual life and hoped to select a project topic that would satisfy both academic and spiritual needs.

During Demarest's course in January, 1991, I spoke with him concerning the possibility of doing a project related to spiritual disciplines. He made several suggestions concerning bibliographic materials and a possible outline for such a project. He also made himself available, at my request, as a resource person and potential reader for my project.

The same week I discussed the idea with Warren Benson, director of the D.Min. program. He was enthusiastic about my subject and suggested that I begin to formulate a proposal.

At this point I discussed the potential project with the elders of my church, Calvary Community Chapel of Lacon, Illinois. They gave their approval to my pursuit of the work. They also approved time, usually allotted for pastor's conferences, to be used for research and writing. This gave me three weeks, per calendar year, to devote almost entirely to project work.

During the summer of 1991 I met with Warren Benson again, this time submitting a preliminary proposal. We also discussed potential mentors and second readers. I decided to request David Larsen as my mentor, and Bruce Demarest as my second reader. Later the same week, I met with Larsen who approved of my topic and agreed to serve as my mentor. Benson contacted Demarest, who consented to be my second reader.

I also began to challenge people in my congregation to take part in my project. I secured the home of a highly committed couple as the site for teaching. The preliminary dates were set as beginning February 25, 1993, and ending May 27, 1993. Fifteen people were personally asked to participate, each being given a somewhat detailed explanation of what would be included in the study and what would be required of them. By November of 1991 I had eleven definite commitments.

In the fall of 1991 I began preliminary research on the subject. I used bibliographies by Demarest, Larsen, Carl Lundquist of Bethel Seminary, and Rich Cornish, student at Denver Seminary, to build a data base.

My formal proposal was submitted in January of 1991. I received confirmation of its acceptance, via phone and letter, by early March.

In April, 1992, I began work in earnest. Most Mondays, for the remainder of the year, were given to research and writing. Three overnight trips were made to Trinity Seminary for the sake of research at Rolfing Library. Two full weeks, one in October, and one in November, were scheduled for study toward the completion of the first three chapters of the project.

In June I sent a set of proposed deadlines to David Larsen, as well as a copy to the D.Min. office. These deadlines, each ahead of official ones, were promptly approved.

During October I recontacted the hostess for the study group and asked her to mark her calendar for the dates involved. An adjustment was made in the previous schedule to avoid conflict with local high school graduations. Preliminary arrangements for child care on meeting nights were discussed. Others who had previously agreed to participate in the project were also recontacted by phone and were given the course schedule.

I also made a content change in my project during this time period. Sensing a need for more objective grounding of the disciplines, I added a lesson on Bible intake, deleting the proposed lesson on secret good works.

More people were personally challenged from August through November, to take part in the project. One elderly woman reacted quite negatively to the invitation. She expressed strong reservations about the disciplines of silence and fasting. She said she felt silence had little use if it was not grounded in the Word of God. She also said she believed fasting was to be done in secret. In addition, she was negative toward the relational aspects of the project. She said she was not much for sharing and that she did not want to hear people in the group discuss the disciplines unless they knew what they were talking about.

In December of 1992, a general invitation to participate in the project was issued to the congregation. It ran for four weeks, yielding one more person for the group. During this same time period four more people, previously invited personally, made commitments to participate. By January 8, 1993, seventeen adults were pledged to the class.

During January of 1993 I finalized child care arrangements. The finished basement of the study's host couple was secured for school-aged children. My own home, in the same subdivision, was committed for a pre-school care center. Sitters were contacted for each site. Payment was to be by voluntary contributions of parents, supplemented when necessary from the church general fund. In late January I ordered a copy of the song book entitled *100 Hymns 100 Choruses: The Greatest Hymns & Praise Choruses of Yesterday & Today* for each couple and single person participating in the study. The plan was to use it in corporate and individual celebration.

Nine days before the first meeting, a form letter was sent to each committed participant. It reminded them of the time and place of the meeting, child care arrangements, and informed them of the cost of the song book. It expressed thanks for their willingness to participate in the group and told them of my excitement over its potential for strengthening our church. I also enlisted their prayer for our time together.

General Profile of Participants

The people involved in the study included eight men and nine women ranging in age from twenty-six to sixty-four years. The age breakdown included five individuals between twenty and thirty, five between thirty-one and forty, four between forty-one and fifty, one in the fifties, and two between sixty and sixty-five.

All the males were employed. Three, although not farmers, had jobs strongly related to agriculture. Two had middle management industrial positions. One was a teacher, one a welder, and one an assembly line foreman.

None of the females were employed outside the home in a full time capacity although six of the nine worked part time. Their jobs included nursing, teaching piano, selling cosmetics, styling hair, and serving as a librarian. Six were predominantly homemakers, concentrating on raising young children. Educationally, eight of the group had received bachelor's degrees, and four more had attended college to some extent. The remaining five had graduated from high school.

In terms of my perception of spiritual maturity, the group was quite varied. Six had the type of lives required of Christian leaders, six were definitely in the process of maturity, and five showed evidence of spiritual lethargy. Twelve of the group members held significant ministry positions at Calvary Community Chapel.

Class Sessions

This section is an account of the fourteen class sessions that I held with my test group. Each session is analyzed briefly as to content, class interaction, and general observations.

Session One

The first class session was held on February 18, 1993. It was given to orienting the group. Some administrative details were handled at the beginning of the period. Several people were enlisted to help. The host of the study agreed to follow up on those absent from class sessions by providing them with notes and explaining them. A woman volunteered to take funds collected for child care to the church treasurer, and to deliver monthly payment checks to the girls providing child care. Another lady agreed to collect the ten dollar fee for hymn books.

Each member of the group chose an index card bearing a number from one to seventeen (the number of participants in the class). This number was to be attached to all surveys and evaluations handed in to me. This method sought to insure confidentiality and to help in the process of analysis.

Ellison's "Spiritual Well-Being Scale" (Appendix B) was administered for the first time.

"A Spiritual Disciplines Personal Experience Record" (Appendix A) was explained next. This is an instrument of my own creation to record frequency of devotional periods and to evaluate devotional experience on a subjective level. Class participants were encouraged to make periodic notes under particular disciplines, waiting until the end of the class to write summaries.

Finally, the course schedule and introductory lesson were presented. The first lesson dealt with an introduction to spirituality, spiritual disciplines, and course procedures. It sought to define spirituality from several spiritual sources. It then defined spiritual disciplines as God-given practices that can aid in the development of spirituality. Some time was also spent distinguishing prescriptive (commanded) disciplines from descriptive (suggested) disciplines. There was good interaction with the material. The group, while earnest, was quick to acknowledge that the disciplines ahead would present a major challenge. But as one older lady commented: "In discipline there is real freedom."

It was interesting to see the group show even more transparency after the formal class period ended. While enjoying refreshments one man told me he had struggled his whole Christian life to maintain a devotional time and that he desired more intimacy with God, and with the people in the study group. Another man shared with those nearby that he had been much more intimate with the Lord as a new believer than at present. A woman expressed some apprehension about fasting. I was encouraged by this interaction as it reinforced my anticipation of spiritual growth through the coursework.

One disappointing aspect of this class was the attendance. A sprained back, a sick baby, and three job-related obligations reduced the expected seventeen participants to eleven. Those present agreed to pray for faithful attendance throughout the study.

Session Two

The evening began with a time of celebration in song and praise. This was to be the first of thirteen times in which we would attempt to learn the discipline informally as a group. Two praise songs set the mood for a few minutes of sharing. Several individuals voiced praise. Two spoke of meaningful evangelistic contacts that God had provided for them. A woman related how a snow storm had provided believers with the opportunity to pray for safety amid a van full of women returning from a shopping trip. I was pleasantly surprised by the openness in the group as I had expected a number of weeks to pass before this would develop. The lesson for the night focused on the need for solitude. After defining the practice, about twenty minutes was spent examining scriptural references. From Matt 14:22–23 the group discerned that Jesus practiced solitude for the purpose of seeking the Father in prayer. I suggested that he also practiced temporary, intentional neglect of people's needs, in order to cultivate relationship with God. From Mark 1:35–38 the group observed that solitude was preparatory to ministry and that people will attempt to place demands on our time with God. In Luke 4:42 and 6:11–13 it was observed that solitude was Jesus' response both to pressure and to the need for a major decision. People easily saw the connection with their own lives. I also pointed out that Jesus had kept what some would call an all night prayer vigil. Gal 1:16–18 yielded the principles that we are to seek God first and not men, and that long periods of time are sometimes required for God to instruct us thoroughly. One woman in the group also noted that the place of our conversion (Damascus for Paul) often holds later significance for devotional life.

Insights from Christian leaders such as Willard, Kempis, Tillich, and Whitney were read and discussed next. We surmised that solitude is positive, freeing, and revealing. With regard to practical matters we discussed dealing with the telephone and how to prepare a place for devotional practices.

Again, the informal time after the meeting yielded good discussion. A man took me aside to share that he had altered his sleeping and work schedules to accommodate a daily period of devotion. To a young man struggling to find quiet at home, I suggested leaving earlier for work and stopping at a scenic spot along the way.

I felt the meeting went well due to the free discussion and the extensive scriptural backing that was present. The group readily accepted the need for the practice and saw its practical benefits for daily life.

I was also very encouraged by the twelve people who attended despite very severe winter weather.

Session Three

Our time together began in celebration. We sang two songs and had a period for praise. Several people participated. One praise was given for the number of people present despite several irreconcilable conflicts. A woman praised the Lord for renewal taking place in her life.

A few minutes were given to the review of the previous lesson on solitude. I felt the group did well in recalling the major purposes of the discipline as suggested by Scripture.

The major focus of the night was on the discipline of journaling. Once the practice was defined, we spent a good deal of time in examining Scripture that supports the general idea. The stones of Josh 4:1–7 were seen as useful in providing a memorial to God's work and as a teaching device for discipling children. Pss 77:11–12 and 103:1–5 were seen as emphasizing intentional remembering of God's deeds on our behalf. The need for a record to muse on was also mentioned. Ps 102:18 reinforced the need to pass on a record of God's faithfulness to future generations. These principles were easily connected with the concept of journaling.

Several quotations from spiritual leaders yielded principles and stimulated further discussion. Benefits of journaling were quoted such as the provision of a personal history, facilitation of self-examination, and flexibility in approach. Benefits were seen as far outweighing dangers.

Discussion brought forth additional insight. One woman, renewing the practice, remarked about what intimacy journaling can promote and noted how God's sovereign care can be traced through entries. Another noted that her old journals show her how much she knew even as a young believer. One man asked, tongue-in-cheek, "you mean you're asking me to rearrange my whole life around a journal?" He, and the rest of the group, easily saw the challenges and the benefits related to the discipline.

Attendance at the meeting was eleven. The hostess of the study walked out the door to a community meeting as the rest of us walked in for the study. One man remarked about the considerable spiritual resistance there seemed to be in our gathering. My wife reminded me afterward of the need for patience and that, despite my thorough challenge to commitment, many in the group would define that differently than I do.

Session Four

The meeting opened with two praise songs, focusing our attention on God and setting the stage for praise. Several men gave praise to the Lord for job related issues. One spoke of having supervised the moving of an entire assembly line without any injuries or property damage. Another thanked the Lord for safety through extensive travel, and for the fact that the cessation of travel had finally allowed him to be present with the study group. As a whole, though, the group was quieter than usual.

A period was spent in reviewing the discipline of journaling, first without notes and then with them. The group recalled that its functions included memorializing God's faithfulness in our lives and tracing our personal development. It was also mentioned that it is not a commanded discipline.

Time was also given to discuss how the personal times of devotion were affecting individuals. One man said that scheduling a regular half hour with the Lord had helped his entire day become more organized, both at work and at home. Spiritual resistance to such time was noted by another person. A lady mentioned that the use of the song book had soothed her at the end of long days with children.

The discipline of silence was introduced as the practice of temporarily ceasing to talk, and of creating an atmosphere of quiet in order to listen to God and reflect on spiritual matters.

Several passages of Scripture that suggested this habit were examined. 1 Kgs 19:11–13 showed that God does speak to his people. Ps 62:5–6 prompted a lot of discussion. The need to wait on God and not to expect Him to arrange his plans around us was expressed. One person noted that when we wait silently, we find our security in God. Isa 30:15 showed that quietness, coupled with repentance, is to be chosen over a panic filled reliance on men. Prov 17:27–28 and Jas 1:19 were seen as showing the need to conserve words and listen to others.

Insights from spiritual leaders showed that to listen to God we need to also be in touch with our own inner lives.

One of my assignments was met with some opposition and engendered considerable discussion. I asked the group members to spend one entire day in silence, listening to God. One lady said, "I have a real problem with that, I may as well go to a monastery." A male member of the group challenged her asking, "would you have a problem if someone offered you a million dollars to do it?" Others wondered how it would affect family relationships and how it could be worked out logistically. I saw this interaction as very healthy and as a sign that the group was becoming more willing to communicate.

I also encouraged the people to allow God to challenge them and to push out their spiritual boundaries.

I felt that two aspects of this session were especially encouraging. Interaction showed that the disciplines were benefitting the group already. The use of a song book in devotions, new to most, was also helping. This meeting was too long, however, and I purposed not to allow other sessions to be so lengthy. Attendance was thirteen.

Session Five

The meeting began with three worship songs as part of our celebration. "As The Deer," "Open Our Eyes Lord," and "Jesus What A Wonder You Are" set the stage for praise. I pointed out that these songs are doctrinally sound and written in the second person to enhance personal interaction with God. Only two people offered praise to God for his work in their lives, considerably less than usual.

Time was spent reviewing the previous week's lesson on silence. The group universally acknowledged problems in quiet listening to God. They noted continual mental interjections and the desire to do the talking in their prayer life with God. One person mentioned that God brought Scripture passages to mind while she was silent. Most had difficulty quieting the mind for more than one minute.

I also asked for feedback on journaling experiences. One woman, having anticipated difficulty due to small children said that it "wasn't too bad." Another said that he was using his to record meaningful verses from sermons. One woman who had fallen out of the habit remarked how glad she was to be renewing it.

The lesson for the evening dealt with fasting. Passages examined were Matt 4:1–11, 6:16–18, 9:14–15, and 11:19; Luke 2:36–37; and Acts 13:1–3 and 14:23. The group members observed that the practice was prevalent during times of temptation, mourning, seeking the Lord's direction, and desire for his blessing on pending service. They also noted that it was not for show before other people. In addition, I pointed out that Jesus' extended fast had been undertaken as a human being, and that his fasting was purposeful rather than ascetic per se.

Insights from spiritual leaders showed that fasting is to be sincere, is often undertaken in time of a major trial or need, and is not for the purpose of a spectacular experience.

I advised the group to skip only one meal when first engaging in the discipline. I also encouraged those who were pregnant or who had medical limitations to avoid the total fast, substituting abstinence from certain foods.

After the session I had a good discussion with a man who was convicted about his irregularity in eating meals. I encouraged him to establish a regular and healthy eating pattern before starting to fast. This, along with the opportunity to encourage those struggling with quietness, were the best aspects of the evening. Attendance was sixteen.

Session Six

The period began with the singing of worship songs and a time of praise. Several group members shared items for which they were thankful. One shared how older Christian co-workers had helped him endure a major leadership shakeup at his place of work. Another told how attentive the children at the Good News Club had been after an otherwise horrendous day. A woman related her positive first experience with fasting.

Time was spent reviewing the practice of fasting. People were able to recall several major points. They remembered that fasting is to be purposeful, and is not ascetic per se. They also recalled that it is often undertaken in time of trial and that it is not for show.

The discipline introduced was Bible intake. It centered on the need to absorb Scripture for the purpose of growing spiritually.

Several passages of Scripture were examined including Jer 15:16, 1 Thess 5:27, 2 Tim 2:15, and 1 Pet 2:1–3. The participants were very active on their observation of these texts. They spent a lot of time with the parallel of "eating the Word" and human ingestion. They saw that Scripture becomes a delight only as one works at it and becomes familiar with it. The study of Scripture was also seen as a stewardship, the neglect of which was shameful. We also spent significant time with the figure of a nursing baby and how it should encourage us toward eagerness in Bible study. The words of spiritual leaders emphasized the need for proper attitudes in approaching the Word, as well as the psychological and social benefits that regular readers often experience.

We discussed how to go about memorizing Scripture, especially 1 Pet 2:1–3, which we would be memorizing together.

Discussion after the class centered on a man's assumption that he could not fulfill the assignment of following a sermon series due to his work schedule. I suggested the use of a portable tape player on his way to work each day. This period also afforded us the added benefit of encouraging a young expectant mother in her parenting abilities.

The encouraging aspects of this meeting were the return to more extensive praise and the benefit from reviewing fasting. The biblical figures of speech used with regard to Bible intake also proved effective. The attendance at the meeting was fourteen.

Session Seven

The time of celebration began with two praise and worship songs. Two of the praises given involved a good report on an expected baby, and the receptivity of a local school administrator to curriculum concerns voiced by Christian parents. The group was a bit quieter than usual during this time.

A short time was spent reviewing the process of Bible intake. I asked the group members what books they had selected for their Bible reading, and what preacher they were following through a series. A few people responded but most evidently had not made their selections yet. I encouraged them to get started in these areas.

The lesson on devotional Bible study was introduced. It was concerned with the need for personal and pointed application of Scripture, while interacting with God.

Scripture was examined first. From Ezra 7:10 the group discerned that study should progress to application and teaching. From Phil 4:9 I emphasized the need to do what we know. A group member added that this is the way to peace. Heb 5:11–14 was used to teach that discerning use of Scripture requires regular practice. As one person said from Jas 1:22–25, "we're kidding ourselves" if we don't apply what we learn.

Insights from spiritual leaders suggested that eagerness and proper attitudes are important in devotional study. The need to record findings was also mentioned.

The greatest portion of time was given to the process of devotional study. Time was spent first emphasizing the need to lay a solid foundation through observation and interpretation. We then worked through Matt 28:18–20 using observational and interpretational questions provided with the lesson.

Before the evening concluded, I made assignments for the next week. With Luke 15:11–32 as the text I assigned eight class members to develop characters related to the narrative. With 2 Cor 11:23–33 as the text, I assigned six class members to describe aspects of Paul's suffering in the first person.

I felt that I spent too much time on scriptural support in this session, time that could have been better spent helping the students work through some example passages with devotional methods. Attendance was fifteen.

Session Eight

The meeting began with a time for written evaluation of the first half of the course (Appendix C). The point was to allow for improvements in my teaching during the second half of the class.

Two songs, seeking God's illumination, and extolling his love, introduced our time of celebration. Several people shared joyous praise. One couple shared that their adoption proceedings for two grade school aged boys in their custody would be finalized within thirty days. A leader of our Good News Club for children praised God for an eight year old girl who had led a classmate to the Lord. A maintenance supervisor expressed thanks that he had discovered other believers within his company, and that he had had an opportunity to share the gospel with a salesman.

The lesson for the evening focused on the use of imagination in Bible study. The class members presented first person viewpoints of the characters of Luke 15:11–32 and of Paul in 2 Cor 11:23–33. Their accounts showed good preparation, including detail and emotion.

Eight people did first person narrative work from Luke 15. The father's house servant commented on the father's goodness and generosity, being careful not to criticize him. A man presumably working with the older son commented on the son's terrible anger and on the father's great tenderness and mercy toward both boys. The pig farmer said he gave the boy what he could during a famine but that it did not bother him too much to see a Jew suffer. A supposed member of the local synagogue said the father was a disgrace and that the son should be disciplined.

Six people portrayed aspects of Paul's sufferings in 2 Cor 11. They spoke of pain from physical beatings and natural disasters. Some evidently had done research and enhanced their parts through it. The spiritual and psychological pressure of the churches was also brought into play.

I conducted this time in interview fashion and tried to draw the participants into dimensions of their characters that they may have overlooked.

A brief period was left in the class to discuss how to appreciate various imagery of the Godhead such as fortress, warrior, shepherd, and comforter. We also discussed how to create concrete images from abstract biblical principles. I also gave some tips on keeping the imagination under control, urging at least some reading of a Bible handbook or dictionary to avoid unjustifiable excesses.

This seemed to be one of our best meetings since it included a varied approach, and involved the students so extensively.

My wife and I invited the group to our home for refreshments after the meeting. I rode with a man who shared about spiritual growth in his life, including early morning vigils and encouragement of discouraged believers. A man at our house shared some work frustrations with me and asked for prayer. All seventeen members of the class were present.

Session Nine

Ellison's Spiritual Well-Being Scale was administered for the second time at the beginning of the class period.

Two songs of consecration began our time of celebration and focused on issues pertinent to the main lesson of the evening. The sharing of praise began with the acknowledgment of God's work through medical technology in the removal of a cancerous tumor of the brain. A man praised God for a concert, given the night before, which focused on the songs taken directly from the Bible. Another gave thanks for God's grace even when we fail badly in the spiritual realm.

I reminded the group that some of the course assignments needed to take place over a period of time, and that they should not wait until toward the end of the class to get started.

We spent a short time reviewing principles from the previous lesson on the use of imagination in Bible study. The group stated that they felt multiple readings of the text were very helpful and that assuming the roles of different characters in the text helped them see a whole different perspective. The process was also seen to aid meditation.

The lesson for the evening, concerned simplicity, the practice of arranging one's time and assets so as to devote them to the one goal of advancing God's kingdom.

From Matt 22:37–39 the group discerned that everything we are and do must be centered on God, and that this should motivate concern for other people as well. Matt 6:20–21, 31–33 yielded the observations that our heart is given to the things we value most, and that what we consider needs may not be such in the eyes of God. I emphasized that money is not evil in itself and that wasted time is a poor stewardship (1 Tim 6:7–10, Eph 5:15–16).

Insights from spiritual leaders yielded several principles. The members of the study saw that simplicity has to be inner-motivated or it will turn to a legalistic duty. They also saw the need to say no to possible commitments, even good ones, in order to concentrate on essential activities.

My assignment to the group was to examine their priorities in the use of time and money, eliminating unnecessary activities and expenditures, while prioritizing good uses of these assets. I also gave them several choices of practical projects from which to gain exposure to the poor of our area.

I felt that I was too dominant in this particular session, spending too much time lecturing. I also felt that a disproportionate amount of time was spent on scriptural support and not enough on practical tips and explanation of the assignment. In addition, I also began to sense some members of the group straining under the assignments. Attendance was a full complement of seventeen.

Session Ten

Our time together began with sharing concerning our experience with the disciplines through the first nine weeks of the class. I felt that the view of the group was very balanced, admitting to spiritual struggle, yet sensing progress in growth. One participant said he was falling behind on assignments but profiting from what he could get done. Another said that he had trouble controlling his imagination as he was attempting to cultivate its use. I encouraged these men not to give up and to do what they could. A woman shared that she was much more aware spiritually than before the study started and that the discipline of recording times of devotion each week had helped. She also said that fasting was new to her and that it was easier than she had thought it would be. In addition, she expressed encouragement that she had conquered desire for food enough to fast. Others gave assent to the idea that spiritual advancement was taking place.

A time of celebration was shorter than usual, consisting of three songs of worship and praise. I was aware of the need to include some better known songs with the new ones in the remainder of the class sessions.

We recited 1 Pet 2:1–3 together, touching on accountability for one of the Bible intake assignments. We also reviewed the basic ideas inherent in simplicity. I was glad to hear a man distinguish it from frugality, saying it was broader. He summed it up nicely saying, "it means we don't junk up our lives." A woman noted that the more she had, the less she wanted to give.

The new discipline for the evening was practicing the presence. I defined this as the experiential recognition of God's presence and care, at any given moment of our existence, as acknowledged by word or thought.

The group brought forth some good insight from the scriptural support. A man said that Ps 139:7–10 had taught him that God holds his hand through life. Ps 27:7–8 yielded the observation that God wants us to seek him and that the desire for fellowship should be mutual. I spent significant time with Ps 63:2, emphasizing that contemplation of God himself, in addition to the traditional practice of petition, is a legitimate form of prayer. The expectation of 1 Thess 5:17 was also seen as fulfilled by the practice under consideration.

The insights from spiritual leaders spurred considerable discussion. A quote from Brother Lawrence raised the question of motivation for seeking God. We saw that we gain strength and joy from him but that he is also worthy of being sought for himself, and his pleasure, alone. We learned from A. W. Tozer that God's omnipresence and the experience of that presence are too often distinct. Other authors gave encouragement to pray always and to teach our children contemplative discipline.

After giving some time to practical tips, the meeting was adjourned in prayer.

I received some good constructive criticism after the meeting. A woman suggested that I needed to be a little more patient when waiting for group interaction. Another said she was disappointed that celebration had been cut short because she had wanted to share a praise.

Nevertheless, I felt this was one of the best sessions. Its frank sharing, significant interaction, and insight from several sources made it a very good group learning experience. Attendance was fifteen.

Session Eleven

Our time together was opened with two songs of celebration extolling the Father's attributes and the Son's work on the cross.

We worked together again on the memorization of 1 Pet 2:1–3.

I oriented our time of sharing around the member's experiences with fasting and personal celebration through song. One person said she had enjoyed singing to the Lord but had never incorporated it into her devotional life before. A man said he had found himself singing spontaneously at work as a result of doing so devotionally, and that his fellow employees had commented on it. A third group member related how she had incorporated it with practicing the presence. While people were slower to share about fasting, some did. A mother shared that her troubled son had been saved two weeks into a fast. A woman testified that her twenty-four and thirty-six hour fasts were much easier than her thirty day abstention from a particular food. She attributed this to "being a sprinter rather than an endurance runner." I told the group that a major conflict I had been mediating had been resolved during the twenty-fifth day of my partial fast.

We spent time reviewing the discipline of practicing the presence. People mentioned that it was a way to pray without ceasing and that it increased awareness of God. One participant said it means realizing that "He's right there." The discipline introduced was confession. I defined it as the practice of admitting, primarily to God and secondarily to people, that our specified thoughts and actions are sin.

A large proportion of time was spent on scriptural support. 1 John 1:8–10 demonstrated that men are sinful, and sinners, in need of cleansing. I emphasized the need for habitual practice of confession. Jas 5:16, with its command to confess to others, generated a lot of healthy discussion. Group members said it enabled believers to help us overcome sin through prayer and accountability. A relatively new convert from Catholicism expressed her anxiety over this. I encouraged her not to overreact to her background and to realize that people cannot grant God's forgiveness. Group members observed from Acts 19:11–19 that confession is often accompanied by outward acts and that it impacts values. From Ps 32:1–5 they saw that sin can be emotionally devastating and that confession can bring relief from negative physical symptoms. A woman said that Satan uses two lies to keep her from confessing: the sin is too small to confess or too big to be forgiven.

Insights from spiritual leaders yielded the observations that the need to confess will never cease, nor will God's compassion. I cautioned the group not to be overly introspective, instead trusting the Holy Spirit to reveal sin through the Scripture.

As part of their assignment I asked them to practice daily confession to God, and to ask a friend to pray for any besetting sin.

I had mixed feelings about this session. I was very encouraged by the growth evidenced during the time of sharing as well as by the good observations during our time of scriptural study. I was unhappy with myself for not allowing time for praise along with the celebration time. In addition, two women made comments quite uncharacteristic of our group in their nature. One was nearly belligerent in insisting that confession was a critical form of prayer and in correcting a misstatement I had made and corrected myself. Another woman suggested that she had reached total perception of her sins and was in the process of confessing them. Each of these comments caught me a bit off guard but I was able to handle them fairly well. Attendance was eleven.

Session Twelve

Two songs of celebration led us into a time of praise. Five different individuals gave glory to the Lord. An industrial management employee gave thanks that he knew a God who forgives sins unlike his Buddhist workmate who has no concept of forgiveness. A young woman also praised God that her militant Catholic mother would be attending the women's spring luncheon hosted by our church.

I spent a couple of minutes reminding people of their assignments with regard to the practice of simplicity. I asked them to consider their budgets, time schedules, and practical exposure assignments related to the less fortunate. No one had yet completed the latter.

Time was given to the review of confession. Group members recalled that it healed relationships with both God and men. They also remembered that it led to better mental health, and that it was a continual process as more and more sins would be revealed by God.

Personal and intercessory prayer was the combined discipline introduced. I defined it as the practice of approaching God, on behalf of ourselves and others, that he might meet the expressed needs.

Several passages of Scripture established the need for the practice. John 16:24 and Heb 4:14–16 dealt with God's invitation to pray. The group observed that Christ wants us to be bold to receive his sympathetic hearing and that God desires joy to result from our praying. 1 John 3:22–23 and 1 John 5:14–15 were given to establish conditions for answered prayer. The group observed that we need to love one another and pray according to God's will to get answers. Phil 4:6–7 and 1 Tim 2:1–2 showed the need to pray about all things, and to include others in our prayer lives. These last two references engendered a rather lively and extended discussion concerning whether there is such a thing as an insignificant subject for prayer. I said I felt some prayers were rather foolish and that our prayer lives should have more intercession and eternal perspective. A woman replied that this discouraged her from intimacy with God and practicing the presence. Another insisted that God was interested in everything in our lives and we should never hesitate to talk to him. A man questioned our mindsets for prayer since we tend to talk so much about ourselves and pray so little for the lost.

Observations from spiritual leaders emphasized that prayer leads to changed lives, that it is helpful to use a prayer list, and that we need to grow beyond crying exclusively for our basic needs.

After giving the group some practical tips I made two assignments related to the study. I asked them to pray through the church directory, two families per devotional time, and to keep a list of prayer answers until the end of the study commitment.

My overall impression of the session was that it achieved its purpose reasonably well. The time of celebration continued to be quite free and transparent. I realized that I need to be careful not to make statements that are unbalanced in their emphasis as the one on "insignificant prayer." At the same time I felt very happy about the frank, yet gentle manner of the group as a whole in discussing disagreements. One woman, however, continued to trouble me with her harsh-toned, dogmatic statements directed to me and others. I realized a need to develop more skill in responding to her and other such individuals. I also saw the need to spend a bit less time on scriptural support and more on insights from leaders and practical tips. Attendance at the meeting was fourteen.

Session Thirteen

The time before the study period was characterized by lively conversation to the extent that we could hardly get started. One man remarked that "you can record in your study that the group has bonded."

Our formal time was begun in celebration. Three worship songs led to a meaningful time of praise in which six group members participated. Praise was given for the completion of a Bible College course, the birth of a new baby, and the impact of a neighborhood women's outreach. The former wife of a deceased pastor praised God for sustaining her while speaking at a banquet for the last church they served together.

Time was spent reviewing the discipline of personal prayer and intercession. The group remembered that there are conditions for prayer and that we may be bold in prayer. The insistence that everything is an acceptable topic for prayer continued.

The discipline presented during this session was celebration. I defined it as the practice of deliberately enjoying God and his blessings, being certain to praise him for all aspects of our lives, while cultivating a carefree and joyous spirit. Since we had been learning about this practice nonformally, through praise and song for the first thirteen weeks of the course, I asked the group what they had gained so far. One person said she had increased her praise while journaling. Overall, I was surprised at how little response there was. I reemphasized the need to be praising God in song during our personal devotional periods so as to integrate our emotions with objective practice.

Numerous passages of Scripture were examined as a basis for the discipline. Eccl 9:7–9 and Neh 8:7–12 were found to encourage happiness and gladness in God's goodness. Enjoyment of food, drink, nice clothing, and perfume were acknowledged as legitimate. Here the discipline was recognized as the safety against extreme applications of the practice of simplicity. Ps 146:1–2 and 150:1–6 affirmed the group's appreciation for song and instrumentation. People also affirmed that, as a church within moderate fundamentalism, we need to beware that we do not limit expression of praise without warrant. The praise of the Lord through dance and loud cymbals got some good play in the discussion. While this interaction was excellent, one woman was very abrasive in her remarks. No sooner had I read my definition of celebration than she said, "I find this term offensive so I don't use it. I never heard it used until five years ago. I celebrate my son's birthdays, when I meet with God I call it worship." I held my ground and said I respected her right to an opinion but that I did indeed think it was an appropriate term to reflect the content of the material being presented.

A significant amount of time was spent with insight from spiritual leaders. Several principles were gleaned. Celebration was seen as keeping us from taking ourselves too seriously and as a medium for reflecting our joy in the Lord. Members also saw that praise should be given by faith, and that God is worthy of it for who He is apart from what He does.

The assignments for the session were to continue singing during devotional times and to consider changes in our attitudes toward the Christian life based on this discipline.

I felt several aspects of this session were positive. The time of sharing was excellent, both in depth and length. I struck a better balance between time spent with scriptural support and with other aspects of the lesson. I was also encouraged by the openness of the people to new worship forms. I was somewhat disappointed that the nonformal emphasis on celebration apparently had not had much impact. I was also concerned that the remarks of the one group member might serve to quench the Spirit's work among us. At the same time, I was satisfied with the tone and content of my response to her. Attendance was fourteen.

Session Fourteen

The meeting began with a second written evaluation of my teaching skills.

Our time of celebration was extended, following two praise songs, as many people shared about God's blessing in their lives. A lady praised God for extended interaction she and her husband had had with a Black Christian couple (our congregation has no African Americans). A man shared that he had been experiencing victory over a food addiction for forty days, and had lost seventeen pounds. A man said his co-worker had noticed more patience in his life in the past three months. He attributed this change in his life to the spiritual disciplines.

After the time of praise, I asked the group to share what disciplines had helped them the most, and which they had struggled with most.

One member said that using the Bible reading schedule I had suggested had really helped. The memorization of hymns was cited as an encouragement. A person who had not been practicing disciplines at all before the class, said getting back to prayer and Bible study had been great.

People were very open about sharing their struggles as well. A lady said she had to really work on practicing the presence, but that she was growing and that this discipline had led naturally into confession. Silence was generally a struggle for the participants. Men, in particular, had difficulty getting started with journaling, but appreciated the results. One said he used a computer, color graphics included. Fasting was also a particular challenge. It was a surprise to me to learn that some people struggled more with the thirty day partial fast than with the shorter, total fasts. One member challenged the idea that fasting needed to be motivated by a deep need. He said such needs are always apparent if we are discerning.

The new material for the evening covered potential benefits and potential dangers inherent in the use of spiritual disciplines. I briefly commented on such potential benefits as spirituality of the heart, production of spiritual fruit, variety of the devotional life, directed approach to the spiritual life, psychological health, and improved corporate worship. Likewise, I addressed potential dangers such as subjectivity, convergence with unorthodox movements, legalism, pride, and privatization.

I thanked all of the group members for their participation and hard work, and especially acknowledged the host couple for their hospitality.

I also encouraged the practice of these disciplines for the four weeks after the course. I reminded them to complete their Spiritual Disciplines Personal Experience Records as well as a third set of Spiritual Well-Being Scales.

I felt this was a good closing session for several reasons. Praise was extended. The group shared frankly about their struggles in the spiritual life. I had time to give perspective on the disciplines by noting potential dangers and benefits. I also was able to encourage them in their growth and to not be overwhelmed by the volume of assignments.

I felt that one aspect could have been better. Again, I struggled with too much material. I should have cut the lesson down somewhat. Nevertheless, I felt that the time was beneficial overall. Attendance was thirteen.

Follow-Up

During the fourth week of independent work, I sent a letter to each individual participant or couple, reminding them that the period of study was about to conclude. I reminded each to complete a Spiritual Benefits Personal Inventory Record, along with a third Spiritual Well-Being Scale. I asked them to hand these to me personally by June 27, 1993.

4

The Project Evaluation

THE PURPOSE of this chapter is to evaluate the fourteen class sessions that I spent teaching a group spiritual disciplines, and to assess the impact of these practices on their individual spiritual lives. I will also comment on personal benefits that I received from practicing the disciplines along with the students.

Class Sessions

This section will deal with the student evaluation of my instruction and my own evaluation of the fourteen class sessions.

Student Evaluation of Class Sessions

The data analyzed in this section was gathered through the administration of a modified form of the document used to evaluate teachers at Moody Bible Institute (Appendix C). The test was administered once during the eighth week of class, and again during the fourteenth week. Numerical coefficients of five (the best rating) down to one were used. Scoring for each major category is represented in the form of first test average/second test average. Major categories evaluated included personal qualities of instructor, teaching effectiveness, ability to relate to subject matter, teacher-student interaction, and tests, measurements, and assignments.

The most favorably evaluated category (4.81/4.75) dealt with my personal qualities as an instructor. Such traits as grooming, confidence, speech habits, and enthusiasm were rated very highly. The least favorable average rating within this category was given with regard to a friendly, winsome disposition (4.24/4.18). While students generally agreed this trait was present, they did not affirm it strongly. My tendency to antithetic thought and expression probably contributed to this relatively low rating. I need to express agreement more often when I can and to be more conscious of projecting the warmth I feel. On the other hand, my willingness to confront, and say the hard thing, may also have contributed to this score.

My teaching effectiveness also received strong affirmation (4.64/4.60). Students gave very high marks for clear objectives, command of subject matter, and skill in presentation. They were less affirming with regard to my variety in teaching methods (4.47/4.29) and my creativity (4.29/4.35). While these do not show student dissatisfaction, they do show room for improvement. Part of the lack of variety may be attributed to the living room setting, which was not conducive to visual aids via overhead projector. Neither did I want to load students down with class presentations on top of their other assignments. Still, I could have used figures in church history as illustrative practitioners of certain disciplines or could have used a guest speaker to deal with one of the subjects. I need to investigate creative methods of teaching, especially as I begin my eleventh year with the same group.

Ability to relate subject matter received slightly less approval (4.50/4.35). While group participants agreed very strongly that I taught within a biblical framework, some would like to see improvement in other aspects of this category. Relating subject matter to other areas of knowledge (4.41/4.18), to student interests (4.24/4.24), and to other student needs (4.41/4.18), together show that I need to give more thought to the integration of the disciplines with life as a whole. Ideally I should relate the disciplines to systematic theology as well as to a competitive game of basketball. I need to spend more time in the future dealing with specific applications of the disciplines as they effect life. This will be a lifetime project. A defect in my class outlines (Appendix D), contributing to this problem, is that they cover too much material each week. I need to exclude some scriptural references and some insights from spiritual leaders, or have the students deal with some of them on their own. When I was rushed, I did not take adequate time to reflect with students on applicational truth. Less material will make for better integration.

Teacher/student interaction (4.48/4.24) appears to be the area where I can stand to improve the most. While the students agreed strongly that I stimulated their own analysis, they would have liked to experience better quality classroom exchange with me. The trait of encouraging questions and discussion (4.76/4.24) was viewed less favorably on the second evaluation. Under "suggestions for improvement," several commented. One student desired "more encouragement for all students to interact." Another commented that "there was not enough time for discussion—a bit rushed." Again, too much material was a significant part of the problem. Less material, more thoroughly discussed and understood, would benefit students more. The trait within this category that students least appreciated concerned fair consideration of other viewpoints (4.13/3.88). The group also varied widely in their evaluation of this point. Five participants strongly agreed that I gave fair consideration and five others marked the moderating "no opinion." One marked "disagree," one of only three such marks I received during the entire evaluation process. I believe several factors are in view here. First, I do need to show more openness to opinions that conflict with mine. I need to be very careful to remain teachable myself and to admit it when another person has a strong argument. Another factor is that I challenged cherished interpretations of certain passages of Scripture, stating that they were not justified by the context. One woman commented that I had "taken something away from her." While I think I could have been more gentle in my approach, I do not regret my insistence on proper interpretation. A third factor may have been my interaction with a very strong-willed individual in the group. This person made comments on my teaching that were sometimes shocking in their bluntness, and so adamant as to virtually defy a reply. At times I handled this poorly. My responses were sometimes also blunt and adamant. In addition, I overreacted on occasion, not recognizing this person's legitimate points as graciously as I should have. Since this student has some admirers in the group, I may have lost some credibility with them at this point. A fourth factor may have been the attempt to cover too much material, leading me to be either too quick with my answers, or impatient with questions.

The final category evaluated was tests, measurements, and assignments (4.44/4.15). The trait dealing with reasonable assignments scored a relatively low (4.18/3.82). Several participants felt overwhelmed with the volume of material, especially as the class progressed. The assignments requiring blocks of time were especially hard for parents with young children. Nevertheless the majority of the class agreed or strongly agreed that assignments were reasonable. One even felt that they were too easy. The evaluation of this factor seemed to be highly related to the student's present family commitments and busyness. Some freely recognized that the problem was mostly their own and that they needed to evaluate priorities. I do not regret the number of disciplines I covered in the study. My aim was to expose students to a broad spectrum of practices, not to make them masters of a small number. Nevertheless, giving fewer assignments within the given disciplines would probably be beneficial.

Overall, I feel very positive about this aspect of the evaluation. The students were highly affirming in general although I also have become aware of several areas in need of improvement.

Self-Evaluation of the Class

This section contains my own evaluation of the time I spent recruiting, organizing, and teaching my people. The reflections will be primarily concerned with areas not dealt with in the project narrative or by student evaluations.

I feel my methods of recruiting were solid. I challenged eighteen individuals personally, sixteen of whom ended up in the class. Only one person entered the group as the result of the general invitation to the congregation. The one individual who complained of being uninformed about class expectations was one I spoke with on the telephone, rather than in person. With the personal challenges issued six months in advance of the class, and a letter of reminder six weeks beforehand, a highly committed group was formed. The general invitation to the congregation also served as insulation against possible accusations of favoritism. The success of this approach confirmed my conviction that the most effective challenges are given face-to-face and confirmed with reminders.

I also feel good about the general administration of the project, especially with regard to delegation of responsibilities. Two nurseries were available for the children of group members. One was at my home and one at the study site. Sitters were contacted, paid, and, when necessary, transported by participants. One member collected money for the song books and gave it to the church treasurer. Two others shared in playing the piano for the time of celebration. One of the students, an elder in the church, accepted the responsibility of meeting with absentees each week to catch them up on material missed. This saved me a good deal of time and potential frustration.

Attendance itself was instructive. I believe the people involved in the study made a sincere effort to come regularly as borne out by an average attendance of eighty-one percent. Five individuals had perfect attendance and only one, due to job conflicts, was present less than nine times. Attendance was best from the fourth week on. This leads me to believe that a prime time for a spring study in our church is from the middle of March until the middle of May. This period avoids late winter weather as well as late spring graduation schedules. In addition, I attribute the good attendance to a clear challenge and explanation of expectations.

The setting of the class in a home was more of an asset than a drawback. It provided a less formal atmosphere than our rented church facility. People were very relaxed and could be comfortably seated. Refreshments were easily available to break the ice. It also presented a mature Christian couple as models of hospitality. One drawback was the lack of teaching aids such as an overhead projector and chalkboard. This did not diminish effectiveness enough to call for a different setting, however.

One unexpected benefit of the class was the excellent interaction before and after sessions. At times it was difficult to get started and people often lingered at the residence long after the study concluded. I found that people opened up to me personally during the latter period, frequently sharing joys, hurts, and frustrations. It convinced me of the need for more informal time with my people.

Spiritual Benefits to Students

This portion of the chapter deals with the perceived benefits of the spiritual disciplines to the students who practiced them. Two documents were used as the sources of written feedback from students. The first is the Spiritual Disciplines Personal Experience Record (Appendix A). This is an instrument of my own creation, designed to evaluate student practice of disciplines and assignments related to them. The second is Ellison's Spiritual Well-Being Scale (Appendix B). It evaluates spiritual and existential well-being.

Personal Experience Record

Each student was asked to keep a record of the number of times spent in devotional practices each week, evaluate personal experience in the twelve disciplines covered, and then respond to a series of summary questions.

The group as a whole found that the greatest encouragement to have a devotional time came from the joy of knowing the Lord personally. A couple cited accountability to a written record. Several others cited personal benefits such as a sense of orderliness, strength for trials, and improved mental health. The major detriments to regular practice were busyness, tiredness, and family responsibilities, particularly with relationship to small children. People flexed their schedules so as to find time with God, utilizing early mornings, late evenings, children's nap times, and even periods in the middle of the night. I see the need in my teaching ministry to encourage people to be very flexible in seeking time with the Lord. I also want to emphasize the joy of knowing the Lord as well as the practical benefits thereof, rather than bludgeoning them with guilt over neglected devotions.

The keys to practicing solitude were finding a quiet time of the day and a familiar spot. People consistently chose well-known locations such as kitchens, patios, and especially bedrooms. A surprising number chose their cars. While many used the outdoors, and wooded areas in particular, these seemed to be the occasional, rather than the usual, places of worship. This leads me to encourage people to establish a regular, comfortable spot in which to seek the Lord, while not discouraging occasional variance.

The practice of silence provided a major challenge for most people. The most frequent description of the experience was "very difficult". Wandering, cluttered minds, and busy schedules were cited as culprits. Others were confused about their thoughts or felt "lazy" when sitting quietly. Better than half the group did not even attempt to spend a day in silence. Despite the struggle, however, perseverance often brought great reward. Many noted that their minds became sharply focused on God. Others said that they became reflective. Sins were brought to mind and confessed, purposes fell into place, and solutions to problems were revealed. Refreshment, calmness, peace, and joy also resulted. Two people spent an entire day in silence and four others spent from two to six and one-half hours. These seemed to experience the benefits listed above most intensely. I plan to encourage believers to practice this discipline and to resist overwhelming busyness. At the same time I want to be clear that all thoughts should be interpreted by, and subject to, the Word. I will also downplay the whole day period of silence and encourage people to use whatever amount of time they can.

Journaling proved to be very beneficial for about two-thirds of the group. One person said: "it has produced the greatest change in my Christian life since it has forced me to face wrong doing." Another said it was difficult because she did not want to reflect upon or remember the present, painful circumstances. Some did not take part in this practice for lack of discipline or for a strong aversion to writing. Those who worked at journaling used a large number of methods. It was employed for recording prayer requests and answers, major victories, reflection on past entries, devotional Bible study, and for sorting out confusing situations in life. It was also used to record what God is like and how he wants his children to be. Individuals developed nuances of the discipline. One kept insights in a pocket book during the work day, transferring them to a master journal in the evening. Others highlighted by using a colored marker on critical entries or by making notations in margins. In one case the journal became the central organizing force for spiritual life. The main thing I learned from this part of the evaluation is to encourage students to be creative and to use the journal as best suits them as individuals. I also intend to encourage nonwriters to use tape recording devices for reflections.

Fasting proved to be a significant challenge for most group members as only a few had practiced the discipline regularly and many had never tried it at all. About one-third of the group did not participate. Two were medically limited, one was pregnant, and a few simply did not make an attempt. Of those who did practice fasting, obstacles were overcome with the result of great personal benefit. Participants acknowledged such impediments as stomach problems, dizziness, shakiness, and craving for food during fasting. Some also struggled with the lack of discipline and unwillingness to deny self. Most, however, were able to fast for one or two meals with relative ease although tolerance thresholds varied. The benefits most often mentioned were increased focus on God, and unusual mental intensity. Students were able to concentrate on God's attributes and to seek him more effectively in prayer. The intensity was most beneficial in Bible study where it aided both understanding and application of texts. Others noticed increased peace, became acutely aware of food addictions, and became less enchanted with food in general. An especially effective assignment was the partial fast. This was to be a thirty day exercise including abstinence from a favorite food, with a specific intercessory prayer substituted. This allowed individuals to have a spiritual focus related to fasting without having to face the rigors of the discipline. I will emphasize this aspect of fasting in the future. I also want to take steps to help remove the fear of this discipline by assuring people that it is not normally a threat to health. At the same time, I want for students to know that they can seek intimacy with God even if they do not fast.

The practice of Bible intake was familiar to most group members. The majority completed the assignment to take two two hour periods for Bible reading. They reported a greater appreciation for the context and unity of Scripture, as well as its difficulty and complexity. One student stated: "It was great. I didn't want to stop, I grew closer to God." Others struggled. One person said he was not used to doing anything for two hours. Most of the class members did read a single book twelve times and grew in their comprehension of the material. The majority, however, did not take the time to follow a preacher regularly on the radio. This surprised me as I assumed that the participants, especially homemakers, would do so. One listened to Joe Stowell and one to Warren Wiersbe. Several opted for the convenience of following my messages with close attention to application. The group as a whole felt overloaded on this assignment, although I feel very good about how much they did. I think a somewhat lessened assignment would increase enjoyment and execution.

Devotional Bible study was to build on the foundation of Bible intake. I was encouraged to see that every student had taken in enough Scripture to make some personal application to life. While most students were vague in their applications, some were quite specific and a few offered extensive evidence of thoughtful study. Members mentioned beneficial guilt, encouragement, increased ability to love, and ability to withstand persecution as results of their personal work. Even though I mentioned the need to be specific in application, most were not. I need to continue to illustrate how to apply the Bible specifically. In the future I would also like to include material that would help incorporate devotional use of Scripture as a foundation for praise.

The use of imagination in Bible study seemed to capture the interest of the group. The number of passages entered into is remarkable. The death of Lazarus, the kenosis, the Lord at the home of Simon the Pharisee, Paul's beatings and imprisonments, the interaction of Euodias and Syntyche, and the crossing of the Red Sea were among those examined. Several students profited from putting themselves in the place of biblical characters and imagining their own responses to various situations. Some, however, wanted to concentrate on Bible intake and not delve into this area. A couple felt that either it was not a high priority or else was a danger to them. I intend to continue emphasis in this area, while emphasizing the need to guide the mind through contextual and cultural study.

The feedback on assignments related to simplicity was revealing. The practical exposure exercise led people to a number of experiences. One participant worked a morning at the local food pantry, while a couple provided food money for a Bolivian seminary student. One person did some of her shopping in an economically struggling part of Peoria.

A young woman began to befriend homeless teens who frequent the area where our church meets. Yet another individual continued rescue mission work. These experiences were life changing as people acknowledged their gratefulness for what they have. At the same time, however, about half the group did not do this assignment. One reason was busyness, a prime enemy of simplicity. I believe another reason was privatization, a major danger to those emphasizing development of the interior life. I need to continue to emphasize that the inner life is to impact our relationships with people. I also asked individuals or couples to evaluate their lives as a whole. Several gave consideration to their use of money. Resolutions included closer evaluation of purchases, giving up magazines, and increasing giving to missions, to the poor, and to the church in general. Others determined to manage their time better, seeking to become less busy. I feel very good about my presentation of this practice and its effects on my people. I know that major change can take place through basic consideration of time and money usage.

Practicing the presence was helpful to my parishioners to an extent that surprised me. One found that it changed the focus of life and gave consistency to his walk with God. Many found it to be a deterrent to sin, especially in the areas of anger and speech. Life, to some, seemed to be richer, less dominated by circumstances. An individual was motivated toward a life of simplicity while two noted better mental, and even better physical, health. The easiest times to practice the presence were found to be worship services, devotional times, periods of silence, and high pressure situations. The period immediately after a sin was difficult since alienation from God was acutely sensed. The discipline was also a great challenge during work hours as self-dependence and selfishness sometimes crept in. I am very encouraged to keep teaching this practice due to its intensely practical nature, and also because it can be used at any time, and in any locale.

Confession of sin to God was universally acknowledged as beneficial. The benefit mentioned most often was a feeling of relief. Closeness to God and humility before other sinful men were also noted. The hardest aspects of this habit were regular practice, repeated confession of habitual sins, and the specific naming of the sins. Confession to men was readily acknowledged as scriptural, but difficult. About one-third of the members did not do this at all. Those who did named fear of rejection as the main hindrance to the act. Recognition of the need to do this prompted some to seek deeper relationships within the congregation. One person said that horizontal confession had helped in fellowship and had provided encouragement. While the practice of confession is easily accepted in theory, I need to stress a couple of things more. I need to continually assure believers that any sin, committed any number of times, will be graciously forgiven by God upon confession. I also need to lay the groundwork for horizontal confession by teaching about Christian relationships as a whole. I want to assure believers that, within solid relationships, other Christians can be trusted with confessions.

Personal and intercessory prayer was easily accepted in theory but the practice was difficult. Most people had a very hard time praying for individuals outside their own families. They admitted to being selfish and lazy. Some said that when they were successful it was because requests were written down on prayer lists or in their journals. One assignment that proved to be beneficial was to pray through our church directory. Most class members attempted to do this. It made people aware of previous neglect, increased their concern for the congregation, and heightened their desire to get to know fellow worshippers. The general failure of my people to pray, however, is a great burden to me since prayer is so fundamental to the Christian life. I need to continue to encourage them in this, particularly in the use of the church directory and other written instruments.

The final discipline taught was celebration. Efforts to incorporate singing into regular devotional times were not always successful, but did bring joy and comfort to those who made a sustained effort. Several in the study said that it became a vital part of practicing the presence. The group singing and testimonies on study nights brought great benefits.

Many felt that singing set the tone for the study, providing focus, setting pace, quieting the soul, and lifting the spirit. While two members felt the singing time was too rigid, and two did not like it at all, the overall feedback was very positive. The testimony time was also well-received. People generally felt that it affirmed their faith, and that it drew them closer to other group members. This discipline was also instructive attitudinally. It showed the need for more grateful hearts. The need for less solemnity, and for more joy and praise, was also recognized. Praise was seen increasingly as a conscious choice, and the ability to celebrate as a mirror of spiritual health. Our celebration taught me several things. First, non-formal learning can be very effective. We learned well as we practiced. Second, celebration is easier for most in a group context. Praise is contagious. Third, singing is vital to both congregational and individual spiritual life and needs to be stressed in my church. Fourth, we need more formal music education to help us read music and to glorify God more effectively with it.

The final section of the Personal Experience Record included summary questions, three of which are considered here. They asked which disciplines were easiest, which were hardest, and which the participants felt they would use for the rest of their lives. In each case they were asked why. Practicing the presence, prayer, and devotional Bible study were identified as easiest. The primary reason given was that prayer disciplines are not restricted to time and place. In the case of Bible study it was relatively easy due to previously established patterns. An overwhelming consensus identified silence, solitude, and fasting as the most difficult disciplines. In the case of the first two, busy, distracted lives and minds were blamed. Many participants did not feel that fasting was urgently important, or else they had physical limitations that prohibited it. When asked what disciplines they felt they would practice in the future, they said journaling, devotional Bible study, Bible intake, and prayer. Several observations spring from these answers. First, my congregation is terribly taxed for time due to small children and career obligations. I need to strongly emphasize and encourage forms of prayer that are not restricted by schedules or locales. Second, I need to encourage parishioners to spend some time in personal

Bible study, even if it cannot be a lot right now. Third, I want to encourage roundedness. It seems that more subjective and emotional individuals lean toward prayer disciplines, while more objective persons do best with biblical studies. I want to nudge people toward disciplines for which they are not naturally inclined, so as to aid their quest for greater balance and maturity. Fourth, I want to encourage realistic expectations for the future. In many cases, schedules will allow more time for devotional life. At the same time priorities will have to be changed. I want to put these things in perspective without placing a legalistic burden on my people. Small amounts of time spent with the Lord are much better than none at all.

Spiritual Well-Being Scale

Students completed Ellison's Spiritual Well-Being scale three times, during the first, ninth, and eighteenth weeks of the course. The scale is designed to measure spiritual well-being via two categories. The first, religious well-being, measures well-being in relation to God. The second, existential well-being, measures a sense of life purpose and life satisfaction (Ellison 1983, 331).

I expected that the participant's perceptions of their spiritual lives would change noticeably during the time of study. I theorized, as suggested by Bruce Demarest, that students would view their spiritual lives quite positively on the first test, less so on the second, with a partial recovery on the third.

The analysis below will consist of observations of general spiritual well-being, followed by consideration of the sub-categories of religious well-being and existential well-being. Observations are of a general nature and I do not lay claim to a formal, statistical validity.

General Spiritual Well-Being

The test asked twenty questions, worth six points each, for a possible total of 120 points. The averages of the three tests, for the seventeen students were 108/111/114 respectively. While these results did not confirm my hypothesis, they were a pleasant surprise. They showed that, on the average, group members improved their spiritual well-being at each juncture of the class. This was actually true of eight members. Two others had identical scores on the first test, while improving on the last. Only two students evaluated their well-being less favorably at the end of the course than at its beginning. In each case the first evaluation had been very high, dropping only slightly on the third. Only two students followed the expected pattern of a drop at the middle test followed by recovery. This would seem to indicate that the disciplines improved people's spiritual well-being sooner than expected, as second tests yielded better results in nine instances, and five more maintained the same level achieved on the first test. This general overview certainly gives indication that the practice of the disciplines impacted the group positively.

Religious Well Being

Religious well-being, or the perceived strength of a relationship to God, was measured by ten questions, worth a total of sixty points. The comparative averages of the three tests were 49/57/59. While eleven members of the group scored fifty-five or higher, even on the first test, there was marked overall improvement through the period of the study. Twelve of seventeen individuals reported a stronger relationship with God. The other five, all of whom scored fifty-nine or sixty on the initial test, maintained their strong bond with God. Notably, not a single person indicated a diminished relationship with the creator. This was a most encouraging result, and speaks strongly for the positive relationship between an active, disciplined, spiritual life and intimacy with God.

Existential Well-Being

This category measures a sense of life purpose and life satisfaction, without specific religious reference. The respective scores on the three tests averaged 52/54/56. The disciplines did not seem to impact this area as much as the former, but improvement was indicated by fourteen of seventeen participants during the study. Three of the students scores increased markedly by seven, nine, and fifteen points. It may be reasonably said that the use of spiritual disciplines does have some positive effect on the perceived satisfaction of practitioners with regard to life in general.

Final Summary of Evaluation

This summary will provide a final overview of the strengths of the study, as well as areas for improvement.

Strengths

Aspects of the study that were positive are listed below:

1. Recruiting methods were sound including personal invitations and follow-up letters.

2. The teaching outlines provided a good mixture of scriptural, expositional, and applicational material that was easy for students to use.

3. The students recognized that I had control of my material, as well as a strong desire to communicate it.

4. The home setting helped create a relaxed atmosphere that stimulated discussion.

5. Delegation of non-teaching functions was very effective.

6. The students confirmed, through testing, that their spiritual well-being had improved.

7. The students were very positive about their learning experiences, and spiritual growth, as measured by the Spiritual Disciplines Personal Experience Record.

8. I advanced personally in my practice of spiritual disciplines, particularly with regard to fasting, journaling, and practicing the presence.

Needed Improvements

The following facets of my study call for improvement:

1. The outlines need to be a bit more brief so that there is adequate time for interaction during class.

2. The assignments need to be somewhat less demanding for a group of laypersons with significant time constraints.

3. I need to use more variety in teaching methods, including more student participation, and perhaps an occasional guest speaker.

4. I need to entertain opposing views, and even arrogant comments, in a more gracious manner, yet while maintaining control. I need to treat all views fairly.

5. I need to be more patient and encouraging with people as they struggle with the disciplines.

6. I need to emphasize God's grace while teaching these practices so that neither legalism, nor discouragement, set in.

Conclusion

The research for, and presentation of, this material has been a thrilling experience for me. I hope to use it for years to come with those of God's people who want to seek him more earnestly.

Appendix A

Spiritual Disciplines
Personal Experience Record

I. Frequency of Devotional Practice

A. Please circle a number for each time you spend at least one-half hour in devotional practices.

Week

1	Course	Introduction		
2	1	2	3	4
3	1	2	3	4
4	1	2	3	4
5	1	2	3	4
6	1	2	3	4
7	1	2	3	4
8	1	2	3	4
9	1	2	3	4
10	1	2	3	4
11	1	2	3	4

12	1	2	3	4
13	1	2	3	4
14	1	2	3	4
15	1	2	3	4
16	1	2	3	4
17	1	2	3	4
18	1	2	3	4

B. What was the greatest encouragement in maintaining regular devotional times during the period of the study?

C. What was most likely to keep you from times of devotion? What changes did you make, if any, to safeguard such times?

II. The Practice of Solitude

A. Where did you go most often for solitude? Why was this an effective place for you? What other places did you use?

III. The Practice of Silence

A. You were asked to spend at least five minutes, twice a week, in silent listening. How did this effect you spiritually and psychologically?

B. What tended to keep you from the experience of silence?

C. What were the main benefits of this practice?

D. You were asked to go one entire day in silence What did you learn from this experience?

IV. The Practice of Journaling

A. You were asked to make journal entries at least twice a week. What was your experience like?

B. What methods of journaling do you consider most beneficial to you? Why?

V. The Practice of Fasting

A. You were asked to fast several times during the course, for various intervals of time, and to use the normal eating period for spiritual disciplines.

1. Describe your experience in each of the three ten hour fasts (lunch skipped).

2. Describe your experience during the twenty-four hour fast (lunch and dinner skipped).

3. Describe your experience during the thirty-six hour fast (breakfast, lunch, and dinner skipped).

4. Describe your thirty day partial fast from a favorite food, while substituting a particular prayer for it.

5. What was the greatest benefit of the practice for you?

VI. The Practice of Bible Intake

    A. What was the effect of your two extended (2 hour) Bible reading sessions?

    B. What books of the Bible did you read through during the course?

VII. The Practice of Devotional Bible Study

    A. What were some of the benefits of concentrating specifically on applicational study?

VIII. The Use of Imagination in Bible Study.

    A. Describe some of the biblical passages that you delved into with a controlled use of imagination.

    B. Describe the biblical imagery that has been most helpful to you.

IX. The Practice of Simplicity

    A. How did the practical exposure assignment affect you?

    B. What changes have you made or are you planning to make?

X. Practicing the Presence (Contemplation)

    A. In what contexts do you find it *easiest* to practice the presence? *Hardest?* Why?

    B. How has this discipline benefitted you during the last eighteen weeks?

XI. The Practice of Confession

    A. How has this practice benefitted you? What is hardest about it?

How do you feel about your times of confession to another person?

XII. The Practice of Personal and Intercessory Prayer

A. How hard is it for you to pray consistently for others? Why do you think this is?

B. How did praying through the CCC directory affect you?

XIII. The Practice of Celebration

A. What has daily singing of spiritual songs done for your life?

B. What is your response to the weekly praise and singing we did within the group?

C. What does this practice teach you about your general attitude toward life?

XIV. Summary Questions

A. Which disciplines did you find easiest to practice? Why?

B. Which disciplines did you find hardest? Why?

C. Which disciplines do you think, realistically, you will use regularly the rest of your life? Why?

D. Did accountability to a group, to practice these disciplines, affect you? If so, how?

E. Were there any benefits from the class you did not anticipate in the beginning?

F. Do you feel that practicing these disciplines, for the last eighteen weeks, has changed or will change your life? Why or why not?

Appendix B

Ellison's Spiritual Well-Being Scale

For each of the following statements note the choice that best indicates the extent of your agreement or disagreement as it describes your personal experience:

SA = Strongly Agree
D = Disagree
MA = Moderately Agree
MD = Moderately Disagree
A = Agree
SD = Strongly Disagree

1. I don't find much satisfaction in private prayer with God.

2. I don't know who I am, where I came from, or where I'm going.

3. I believe that God loves me and cares about me.

4. I feel that life is a positive experience.

5. I believe that God is impersonal and not interested in my daily situations.

6. I feel unsettled about my future.

7. I have a personally meaningful relationship with God.

8. I feel very fulfilled and satisfied with life.

9. I don't get much personal strength and support from my God.

10. I feel a sense of well-being about the direction my life is headed in.

11. I believe that God is concerned about my problems.

12. I don't enjoy much about life.

13. I don't have a personally satisfying relationship with God.

14. I feel good about my future.

15. My relationship with God helps me not to feel lonely.

16. I feel that life is full of conflict and unhappiness.

17. I feel most fulfilled when I'm in close communion with God.

18. Life doesn't have much meaning.

19. My relation with God contributes to my sense of well-being.

20. I believe there is some real purpose for my life.

Please note that in the actual document used with the test group the scale symbols SA, MA, A, D, MD, and SD follow each question.

Appendix C

Evaluation of Dan Green's Instruction

Please rate the following categories in the instruction you have received in this course using this legend:

5 = Strongly Agree
4 = Agree
3 = No opinion
2 = Disagree
1 = Strongly Disagree

Please circle the appropriate rating number and return to instructor.

Personal Qualities of Instructor

1. Is well groomed	5 4 3 2 1
2. Has self confidence	5 4 3 2 1
3. Has a friendly winsome disposition	5 4 3 2 1
4. Seems spiritually motivated	5 4 3 2 1
5. Practices good speech habits	5 4 3 2 1
6. Has good voice control	5 4 3 2 1
7. Is enthusiastic about subject	5 4 3 2 1

Teaching Effectiveness

8. Has clearly defined objectives for the course	5 4 3 2 1
9. Has command of subject matter	5 4 3 2 1
10. Is organized in his presentation	5 4 3 2 1
11. Is skillful in his presentation	5 4 3 2 1
12. Uses variety in teaching methods	5 4 3 2 1
and instructional materials when possible	5 4 3 2 1
13. Is creative in teaching	5 4 3 2 1
14. Involves students in a variety of resources	
related to the subject	5 4 3 2 1

Appendix C

Ability to Relate to Subject Matter

    15. Relates subject to other areas of knowledge   5 4 3 2 1

    16. Applies subject matter to current student
            spiritual needs and problems when applicable   5 4 3 2 1

    17. Relates subject to personal interests of students
            when applicable   5 4 3 2 1

    18. Teaches subject matter within biblical framework   5 4 3 2 1

Teacher/Student Interaction

    19. Encourages questions and discussions   5 4 3 2 1

    20. Gives fair consideration of other viewpoints   5 4 3 2 1

    21. Stimulates students to analyze
            subject matter carefully   5 4 3 2 1

    22. Responds to student feedback   5 4 3 2 1

    23. Has students apply concepts to
            demonstrate understanding   5 4 3 2 1

    24. Shows genuine interest in students as individuals   5 4 3 2 1

Tests, Measurements and Assignments

    25. Makes reasonable requirements in assignments   5 4 3 2 1

    26. Assigns projects meaningful to the objectives
            of the course   5 4 3 2 1

Suggestions for Improvement:

Appendix D

Spiritual Disciplines
Schedule and Lessons

Date	Schedule
February 18	Introduction to Spirituality, Spiritual Disciplines, and Course Procedures
February 25	Solitude
March 4	Journaling
March 11	Silence
March 18	Fasting
March 25	Bible Intake
April 1	Devotional Bible Study
April 8	The Use of Imagination in Bible Study
April 15	Simplicity
April 22	Practicing the Presence
April 29	Confession (vertical and horizontal)
May 6	Personal and Intercessory Prayer
May 13	Celebration
May 20	Final Summary and Sharing

Introduction to Spirituality, Spiritual Disciplines and Course Procedures

I. **Spirituality: What it Is**

A. "Spirituality is simply the holistic quality of human life as it was meant to be, at the center of which is our relation to God" (Dallas Willard, *The Spirit of the Disciplines*, p. 77).

B. "In 1 Corinthians 10:23, 24 I am told that my longing in love should be to seek the other man's good and not just my own . . .

These are the areas of true spirituality. These are the areas of true Christian living. They are not basically external; they are internal, they are deep; they go down into the areas of our lives we like to hide from ourselves. The inward area is the first place of loss of true Christian life, of true spirituality, and the outward sinful act is the result. If we can only get hold of this—that the internal is basic, the external is always merely the result—it will be a tremendous starting place. . . .

And having come this far, true spirituality—the Christian life—flows on into the total culture" (Francis Schaeffer, *True Spirituality*, p. 12–13, 180).

C. "The life of the Christian ought to be adorned with all virtues, that he may be inwardly what he outwardly appeareth to men" (Thomas á Kempis, The Imitation of Christ, I:XIX).

D. Summary—Spirituality is the result of taking what we say we believe, and making it a matter of the heart, so that it deeply and positively affects our relationships with God and fellow men.

II. **How classical spiritual disciplines relate to spirituality**

A. "The inner righteousness we seek is not something that is poured on our heads. God has ordained the Disciplines of the spiritual life as the means by which we place ourselves where he can bless us. . . . spiritual growth is the purpose of the disciplines." (Richard Foster, *Celebration of Discipline*, p. 7–8).

B. "I will maintain that the only road to Christian maturity and godliness (a biblical term synonymous with Christlikeness and holiness) passes through the practice of the Spiritual Disciplines. I will emphasize that Godliness is the goal of the Disciplines, and when we remember this, the spiritual disciplines become a delight instead of a drudgery. . . . By them we place ourselves before God for Him to work in us" (Donald Whitney, *Spiritual Disciplines for the Christian Life*, p. 14–15).

C. "Discipline yourself for the purpose of godliness . . . since it holds promise for the present life and also for the life to come" (1 Tim 4:7–8).

III. Division of Disciplines

A. Explicit—those which are clearly commanded

1. Bible study
2. Meditation
3. Petition
4. Confession
5. Intercession

B. Implicit—those which are assumed as necessary or helpful

1. Solitude
2. Silence
3. Fasting
4. Journaling
5. Practicing the presence
6. Simplicity

IV. Course materials

A. Bible

B. Journal

C. Hymn book

D. Weekly notes

V.   **Procedures**

   A. Class schedule

   B. Weekly routine
      1. Individual
      2. Group

   C. Spiritual Disciplines Experience Record
      1. During class (14 weeks)
      2. After class (4 weeks!)
      3. Due June 27th

   D. Evaluation
      1. Spiritual well-being scale—anonymous number
      2. Teacher competency—anonymous number

Solitude

I.   **Definition**

   The practice of seeking aloneness, in a place free of noise and distractions, for the sake of spiritual reflection and communion with God.

II.   **Biblical Support**

   A. Matthew 14:22–23

   B. Mark 1:35–38

   C. Luke 4:42, 6:11–13

   D. Galatians 1:16–17

III. **Insight From Spiritual Leaders**

   A. "Solitude frees us, actually. This above all explains its primacy and priority among the disciplines. The normal course of day-to-day human interactions locks us into patterns of feeling, thought and action that are geared to a world set against God. Nothing but solitude can allow the development of a freedom from the ingrained behaviors that hinder our integration into God's order" (Dallas Willard, *The Spirit of the Disciplines*, p. 160).

B. The wisdom of our language has grasped these two sides of man's being alone. It has created the word loneliness in order to emphasize the pain of being alone, and it has created the word solitude in order to emphasize the glory of being alone" (Paul Tillich, "Let Us Dare to Have Solitude," in *Quarterly Review*, p. 10–11).

C. "One hath said, 'As oft as I have gone among men, so oft have I returned less a man'. . . . He, therefore, that seeketh to reach that which is hidden and spiritual, must go with Jesus 'apart from the multitude'. . . . Shut thy door upon thee, and call unto thyself Jesus thy beloved. Remain with Him in thy chamber, for thou shalt not elsewhere find so great peace. If thou hadst not gone forth nor listened to vain talk, thou hadst better kept thyself in good peace" (Thomas á Kempis, *The Imitation of Christ*, I:XX:7).

D. "What we are in them (solitudes), that we are indeed, and no more. They are either the best or the worst of our times, wherein the principle that is predominant in us will show and act itself" (John Owen, in Donald Whitney's *Spiritual Disciplines for the Christian Life*, p. 183).

IV. Practical tips

A. Find a regular place to meet with the Lord.

B. Equip your place with a Bible, hymn book, journal, and pen.

C. Deal with the phone. Take it off the hook or turn on the answering machine. You have an appointment.

D. Find some other spots to retreat to periodically. These may include a park, a spot in the woods, or a lakeside.

V. **Assignment**

    A. During the eighteen weeks of the course, meet alone with the Lord four times a week, for at least one-half hour each time.

    B. Record the number of times you meet with the Lord.

    C. Summarize your experience on your Spiritual Disciplines Experience Record.

Journaling

I. **Definition**

    The practice of keeping a written record of one's spiritual journey, including personal interaction and encounters, with God and people.

II. **Biblical Support**

    A. Joshua 4:1–7

    B. Psalm 77:11–12

    C. Psalm 103:1–5

    D. Psalm 102:18

III. **Insights From Spiritual Leaders**

    A. "A journal is a record of what God is doing in our lives, the events and happenings God brings into lives . . . it is to us what history is to the world. . . . It is a record of inner life, its emotions and graces. It is a spiritual and emotional context for life" (Bruce Demarest, T.E.D.S. lectures, winter 1991).

    B. "Journaling can be more than simply a means to 'think things through'; it can be a spiritual discipline. One person may journal in response to Bible study. Another may take a meditational walk or have a time of silence and then record the thoughts and prayer that occurred during that time. Someone else may record daily events and then see the hand of God in that dailiness.

Journaling can be a freeing spiritual discipline because there is no set 'right' method for spiritual growth, but a variety of approaches that have in common pen, paper, and the desire to come closer to God in the writing" (Anne Broyles, *Journaling: A Spirit Journey*, p. 13).

C. "When I first began to think of this subject, various objections appeared to me to lie against diary writing altogether. It would give room for spiritual pride; it led persons to measure themselves by themselves; and as it is not easy to determine between the motions of the spirit and the natural outworkings of the unrenewed conscience or the artifices of the Deceiver, there is a danger of forming incorrect judgments. These and other reasons kept me a length of time from determining for the thing. Of late I have got over these objections entirely, and am now of the opinion that such a record may be of much service to an individual to furnish him with matter for prayer and self-examination, and to be a monument to God's faithfulness" (Thomas Houston in Edward Donnelly's *The Diary of Thomas Houston of Knockbracken*, p. 11–12).

D. "Most of us . . . live unexamined lives. We repeat the same errors day after day. We don't learn much from the decisions we make, whether they are good or bad. We don't know why we're here or where we're going. One benefit of journaling is to force us to examine our lives" (Bill Hybels, *Too Busy Not to Pray*, p. 103).

IV. Practical Tips

A. Choose a journal. You may use a simple spiral notebook, or a composition book with a soft binding. Perhaps you will prefer a more formal type that can be purchased at the local Christian bookstore.

B. Use the journal as a record book of what God reveals to you through other spiritual disciplines and through daily living.

C. Interact, with full honesty, with God. Write about aspirations, fears, sins, struggles, and relationships with people.

D. Keep its contents private, except for occasional insights you wish to share with an intimate friend or relative.

E. Highlight in red for later reference. Use symbols to mark significant insights in the margins:

Q = something revealed during quietness
I = a meaningful biblical image
P = prayer answer
B = biblical insight
F = frustration
S = song, etc.

F. Refer to the journal as a means of encouragement, accountability, and perspective.

V. Assignment

A. Make at least two journal entries a week, for eighteen weeks.

B. Fill out the Spiritual Disciplines Personal Experience Record.

Silence

I. Definition

The practice of temporarily ceasing to talk, and of creating an atmosphere of quiet in order to listen to God and to reflect on spiritual matters.

II. Biblical Support

A. 1 Kings 19:11–12

B. Psalm 62:5–6

C. Isaiah 30:15

D. Lamentations 3:24–26

E. Proverbs 17:27–28

F. James 1:19

III. Insights From Spiritual Leaders

A. "There is another, equally important way of praying in which a person becomes silent and tries to listen instead of speaking. Instead of picking up a familiar lead and speaking about the things that all of us feel are needed, one tries to become still. One's effort is to be silent enough to hear, first, the deepest needs of one's own heart, and then the prompting of the creative Spirit in whatever direction it may indicate" (Morton Kelsey, *The Other Side of Silence*, p. 93).

B. "In silence we close off our souls from 'sounds,' whether those sounds be noise, music, or words. Total silence is rare, and what we today call 'quiet' usually only amounts to a little less noise. Many people have never experienced silence and do not even know that they do not know what it is. Our households and offices are filled with the whirling, buzzing, murmuring, chattering, and whining of the multiple contraptions that are supposed to make life easier. Their noise comforts us in some curious way. In fact, we find complete silence shocking because it leaves the impression that nothing is happening. In a go-go world such as ours, what could be worse than that!" (Dallas Willard, *The Spirit of the Disciplines*, p. 163).

C. "In silence we learn to rely more on God's control in situations where we would normally feel compelled to speak, or to speak too much. We find out that He is able to manage situations in which we once thought our input was indispensable. The skills of observation and listening are also sharpened in those who practice silence and solitude so that when they do speak there's more of a freshness and depth to their words" (Donald Whitney, *Spiritual Disciplines for the Christian Life*, p. 185).

D. "Prayer is answering speech. The first word is God's word. Prayer is a human word and never the first word, never the initiating and

shaping word, simply because we are never first, never primary"
(Eugene H. Peterson, Working the Angles, p. 33).

IV. Practical Tips

A. Find a quiet spot in the house or elsewhere. Use a pair of ear-plugs if necessary.

B. Turn off the television, radio, and stereo. Take the phone off the hook or turn on the answering machine.

C. Cast guilt concerning the past and anxieties concerning the future on God. Concentrate on being quiet now.

D. Invite God to work within you and ask him to safeguard your time together from spiritual deception.

E. Record impressions in writing for later reference. Be sure to check them against Scripture.

F. In relationship with both God and people, listen more, and talk less.

G. Set aside time periodically for quiet reflection.

V. Assignment

A. Spend at least five minutes per day, twice a week, listening to God.

B. Spend one entire day without speaking, and as quietly as possible.

C. Record your experience on your personal experience record.

Fasting

I. **Definition**

The practice of abstaining from food temporarily, in order to concentrate more fully on spiritual pursuits.

II. **Scriptural Support**

A. Matthew 4:1–11, 11:19

B. Matthew 6:16–18

C. Matthew 9:14–15

D. Luke 2:36–37

E. Acts 13:1–3, 14:23

III. **Insights From Spiritual Leaders**

A. "The credibility of fasting is not in the abstention from food but in the sincerity of the person who manifests his faith by withholding himself from food. . . . When a person believes that God will be honored by the dedication of his body, the time spent in prayer, and the abstinence from food, his fasting becomes an act of faith" (Jerry Falwell, *Fasting: What the Bible Teaches*, p. 30).

B. "Fasting then is a legitimate response to dangers, trials, heartaches, or sorrows. . . . In times of physical or spiritual need Christians realize their inadequacy and in humility and repentance look to the Lord. These emotions may be demonstrated by private fasting. On the other hand, if there is no felt need of a serious nature, fasting does not seem to be required of believers" (Curtis Mitchell, *The Practice of Fasting in the New Testament*, p. 469).

C. "God may give unusual manifestations of His presence in such times, but we are not to seek after these as though they were the essential ingredient. The value of a fast is not to be judged by how much there is of the spectacular or the dynamic, but how much there is of solid lasting gain for the kingdom of God" (Arthur Wallis, *God's Chosen Fast*, p. 118–119).

D. "In a time when one of the dominant sins in America is gluttony, it is salutary to do without food for short periods in the year in order to draw close to God in prayer. Fasting also sets us free for service to our neighbor. By skipping a meal every now and then, we can use this time to visit or pray for the sick; the money that we save can be used to help someone in dire distress. . . . When fasting becomes normative or fashionable, then obviously it can no longer be considered a work of piety. But to fast and pray in secret—this is the way of Christian discipleship" (Donald Bloesch, *The Crisis of Piety*, p. 57).

IV. Practical Tips

A. Determine a spiritual purpose for each fast. Keep in mind that the point is not to promote an ascetic ideal or to gain physical benefits.

B. Begin with moderation. Skip only one meal at first.

C. Commit the time to prayer, Bible study, counseling, service, or another spiritual pursuit as you have determined.

D. Drink several glasses of water per day.

E. When breaking a longer fast, begin with juices or a light meal consisting of fruit or vegetables.

F. Do not practice total fasting if you are diabetic, on medication which would be adversely affected, or pregnant. In such cases abstinence from a certain food may serve a helpful purpose.

V. Assignment

A. During the remaining thirteen weeks of the course, fast five times.

B. Observe three ten hour fasts (lunch skipped), one twenty-four hour fast (lunch and dinner skipped) and one thirty-six hour fast(breakfast, lunch, and dinner skipped).

C. Observe a thirty day partial fast (abstinence from a favorite food or food group).

D. For each fast, identify a spiritual purpose.

E. Record your experience on the Spiritual Disciplines Spiritual Experience Record.

Bible Intake

I. **Definition**

The practice of concentrated absorption of Scripture, through various means, as a catalyst for spiritual growth.

II. **Scriptural Support**

A. Jeremiah 15:16

B. 1 Thessalonians 5:27

C. 2 Timothy 2:15

D. 1 Peter 2:1–3

III. **Insights From Spiritual Leaders**

A. "It's hard for us to imagine that many of us have more Bibles in our homes than entire churches have in some Third-World situations. But it's one thing to be unfamiliar with Scripture when you don't own a Bible; it's another thing when you have a bookshelf full. . . . No spiritual discipline is more important than the intake of God's Word. Nothing can substitute for it. There is simply no healthy Christian life apart from the diet of the milk and meat of Scripture" (Donald Whitney, *Spiritual Disciplines for the Christian Life*, p. 24).

B. Helpful Attitudes

The Positive: I want to learn how to study the Bible. No doubt I will have trouble learning some of the Bible study skills. I am sure there will be things in the Bible I'll not understand. But I believe that through the help of the Holy Spirit I too can learn how to gain insight into God's Word.

The Receptive: God asks of me only an open heart and an open mind so that he can reveal himself and his truths to me. I don't have to understand everything.

The Expectant: I am coming to God's Word to let him speak to me. It is good to know that I don't have to inject ideas into my reading or to try to squeeze truths out of it. As I study and pray, I believe that the message in any Scripture passage will unfold itself to me.

The Faithful: I cannot expect much from Bible study unless I am willing to invest some energy and discipline in the study. I realize that God has placed a price on his Word: faithfulness and diligence in study. If I only scratch the surface, my reward is a few crumbs. If I dig deeply into the Word, my reward will be rich treasures (Oletta Wald, *The Joy of Discovery*, p. 11–12).

C. "Regular Bible reading and meditation is associated with a generally stable emotional life and the ability to ride out shocks of various kinds . . . It is evident that continuing Christian discipleship, and particularly serious attention to the Bible and its message on a regular basis, does motivate Christians across the board of personal and social concerns, and may well be the lever to reverse the trend of a society that apparently is becoming more Christian in religious persuasion and less just in social and personal practice" (Harold O. J. Brown, *What's the Connection Between Faith and Works?*, p. 28–29).

IV. Practical Tips

A. Remember that God's Word is a priceless treasure. It is an inerrant guide to life which must be revered and applied.

B. Observe passages of Scripture through inquiry. Ask questions about the text: who?, what?, why?, when?, where?, how many? Also observe repetition, comparisons, and contrasts.

C. Listen closely to preaching. What is the preacher's main point? His subpoints?

D. Set goals for how often you will read the Bible and how much you want to cover the remainder of the year.

E. When memorizing Scripture, work on one phrase at a time, mulling it over and over. Build the verse gradually. Try to understand the context of the verse.

V. Assignment

A. Choose *one* of the following books to get to know well— Philippians, Colossians, 2 Timothy, or 1 Peter. Read it at least twelve times in the remaining twelve weeks of the class.

B. Follow a preacher through a series on the radio, by tape, or in church.

C. Twice during the course, spend two hours in uninterrupted Bible reading.

D. Memorize 1 Peter 2:1–3.

E. Record your experience on your Spiritual Disciplines Personal Experience Record.

Devotional Bible Study

I. Definition

The practice of studying Scripture with the major emphases on personal application, and on interaction with God about that application.

II. Scriptural Support

A. Ezra 7:10

B. Philippians 4:9

C. Hebrews 5:11–14

D. James 1:22–25

III. Insights From Spiritual Leaders

A. "Devotional study is not so much a technique as a spirit. It is the spirit of eagerness which seeks the mind of God; it is the spirit of humility which listens readily to the voice of God; it is the spirit of adventure which pursues earnestly the will of God; it is the spirit of adoration which rests in the presence of God" (Merrill C. Tenney, *Galatians*, p. 189–190).

B. "It is in the pursuance of this method that Satan will raise his greatest opposition. He may not be too concerned when the believer endeavors to study the Bible from the scientific, philosophical, or psychological standpoint; but when he starts to apply the Word to his personal life in order to have a more victorious life and thereby to present a more effective witness, the story is quite different. The Evil One will do all in his power to prevent such an eventuality, and the believer will soon discover increasing temptation coming his way to spend his time on things other than personal Bible study" (Howard F. Vos, *Effective Bible Study*, p. 172–173).

C. "Unless we apply what we have learned, our study has not accomplished its primary purpose, even though we may have gained much intellectual knowledge. . . . In fact it is a very dangerous thing to study the Bible and not be open to its message. The Word of God is power. It either penetrates hearts or hardens hearts. The person who is not open to the Holy Spirit as he speaks through the Word can consciously or unconsciously be rejecting its truth, and in the process harden his heart" (Oletta Wald, *The Joy of Discovery*, p. 89).

D. "Whatever the approach the believer chooses in his devotional study of the Bible, it is the opinion of the writer that such a development will be much more effective when finds are recorded, because divine claims on the individual life make a greater impact when they appear in ink or type than they do when they merely pass through the mind for a fleeting moment. Moreover, devotional blessings will then be preserved as a reminder to the heart of that which God has spoken in the past" (Howard F. Vos, Effective Bible Study, p. 178).

IV. Practical Tips

A. Pick a passage of Scripture. Begin reading.

B. Spend adequate time in observation and interpretation before moving to application.

C. Meditate (think on it) at selected points.

D. Ask the following questions. (Grace Saxe in Vos, p. 176)

1. What does the passage teach about God?

2. Is there an example for me to follow?

3. Is there an error for me to avoid?

4. Is there a duty for me to perform?

5. Is there a promise for me to claim?

6. Is there a prayer for me to echo?

E. Pray over the passage. Ask God how it should affect you.

F. Begin reading again until you want to stop at another verse. Repeat the cycle.

G. Example passages

1. Ephesians 4:31–32

2. Philippians 4:6–9

V. Assignment

A. You have chosen a book to read twelve times. Work through this same book applicationally in as much depth as you have time for.

B. Write down *specific* applications.

C. Record your general findings on your "Spiritual Experience Personal Inventory Record."

The Use of Imagination in Bible Study

I. Definition

The practice of using the imagination to create mental pictures, so as to enter into biblical scenes or to bring concreteness to abstract concepts.

II. Insights From Spiritual Leaders

A. "Using the imagination, one can step into the events recorded in the New Testament or into the stories told by Jesus. One can be present at the birth in Bethlehem, at the stilling of the sea or the feeding of the five thousand, at the foot washing; the crucifixion or at the various resurrection appearances. . . . We can also step into the pages of the Old Testament with the help of imagination, particularly the Psalms which express the whole range of human emotion and every agony of dereliction. The Psalms reassure us that we can bring any pain or fear to God. One can relive Elijah's journey into the desert, or see him taken up in the chariot of fire as Elisha accepts his mantle. . . . We can suffer with Job and out of our own agony identify with his struggle, or we can stand beside the burning bush with Moses or walk with Jacob or Joseph or Abraham" (Morton Kelsey, *The Other Side of Silence*, p. 188, 214).

B. "Imaginatively reconstruct a typical family belonging to the jailer. Here they are, Christians in Philippi. It must have been difficult. Clearly there was antagonism to the believers in Jesus. An ugly situation had developed. Paul and Silas had been dragged into the marketplace before the authorities. Philippi was a Roman colony; there weren't many Jews there to begin with. Being a gentile who had responded to the message of a Jewish man must have been an awkward thing. Reconstruct what it was like to be a Philippian jailer who was a Christian. Imagine what it was like for his wife and his son and his daughter—and perhaps for his servants. It would be clear that being a Christian was not easy for these people" (Harold Freeman, *Variety In Biblical Preaching*, p. 132).

C. The many biblical images help us sense who he is and help us warm to his presence: shepherd, gardener, father, husband, mother hen, fortress, eagle's wings, vine. And many symbols speak of what he has done for us: shewbread, altar, sacrifice, bread, door, veil, high priest, prophet, king. These images and literally hundreds of others are food for our times of being with God, for they nourish prayer of the heart and our awareness of who God is. How important it is that we use God's Word; not simply as a source of doctrine but as a love letter that reveals our beloved and draws us deeper and deeper into his presence" (Lawrence O. Richards, *A Practical Theology of Spirituality*, p. 108).

D. "Some have objected to using the imagination out of concern that it is untrustworthy and could even be used by the Evil One. There is good reason for concern, for the imagination, like all our faculties, has participated in the Fall. But just as we can believe that God can take our reason (fallen as it is) and sanctify it and use it for his good purposes, so we believe he can sanctify the imagination and use it for his good purposes. Of course, the imagination can be distorted by Satan, but then so can all our faculties. God created us with an imagination, and as Lord of his creation he can and does redeem it and use it for the work of the kingdom of God" (Richard J. Foster, *Celebration of Discipline*, p. 25–26).

III. Examples of Biblical Imaging

A. Imagery of the Godhead

1. Fortress (Psalm 1:2)

2. Warrior (Exodus 15:3)

3. Shepherd (John 10:11)

4. Comforter (John 14:26)

B. Imagination in Passages

1. Luke 15:11–32: perspectives of different characters

2. 2 Corinthians 11:23–33: physical and emotional sensations

C. Creating images of biblical concepts

1. Gentleness: a powerful stallion under the control of his master.

2. Purity: a centurion guarding a maiden (Charles Swindoll, *Strengthening Your Grip*, p. 55).

3. Yielding burdens: handing a particular burden to God, as in Isaiah 55:22.

IV. Practical Tips

A. Read the description of a particular biblical scene several times, each time taking the perspective of a different character.

B. Read a Bible encyclopedia or Bible handbook to find out more about scriptural images and to safeguard the imaginative process.

C. Allow time for the mind to mull over the accumulated information.

V. Assignment

    A. Spend some more time developing the characters of Luke 15:11–32 or the sensations of 2 Corinthians 11:23–33.

    B. Investigate several of the images present in the book you are reading twelve times.

    C. Make personal applications from your findings in A. and B.

    D. Record your findings on you Spiritual Disciplines Personal Experience Record.

Simplicity

I. Definition

    The practice of arranging one's time and assets so as to devote them to the one goal of advancing God's kingdom.

II. Scriptural Support

    A. Matthew 22:37–39

    B. Matthew 6:20–21, 31–34

    C. 1 Timothy 6:7–10

    D. Ephesians 5:15–16

    E. Matthew 28:18–20

III. Insights From Spiritual Leaders

    A. "The Christian Discipline of simplicity is an inward reality that results in an outward life-style. Both the inward and the outward aspects of simplicity are essential. We deceive ourselves if we believe we can possess the inward reality without its having a profound effect on how we live. To attempt to arrange an outward life-style of simplicity without the inward reality leads to deadly legalism" (Richard Foster, *Celebration of Discipline*, p. 80).

B. "We are not integrated. We are distraught. We feel honestly the pull of many obligations and try to fulfill them all. And we are unhappy, uneasy, strained, oppressed, and fearful we shall be shallow. For over the margins of life comes a whisper, a faint call, a premonition of richer living which we know we are passing by. Strained by the very mad pace of our daily outer burdens, we are further strained by an inward uneasiness, because we have hints that there is a way of life vastly richer and deeper than all this hurried existence, a life of unhurried serenity and peace and power. If only we could slip over into that Center! If only we could find the Silence which is the source of sound! We have seen and known some people who seem to have found this deep Center of living, where the fretful calls of life are integrated, where No as well as Yes can be said with confidence" (Thomas Kelly, *A Testament of Devotion*, p. 115–116).

C. "You see, on some level we think we have a right to do what we want when we want. Our goal is to have as much happiness as possible and to avoid pain at all costs (which is precisely what causes most of the pain in the world). So we rush around frantically grabbing hold of the things we imagine we want and even more frantically avoiding anything that might be unpleasant—and we die of colitis and high blood pressure and misery" (John Alexander, "A Rich, Full Life," p. 14).

IV. Assignment

A. Examine the use of your time. Does it center onGod? Are you involved in too many activities? Too few? Can you say no? Begin to eliminate unnecessary commitments.

B. Examine the use of your money. Do you have a budget? Does your spending reflect frugality? Does your giving honor God?

C. Do at least one of the following as a practical exposure assignment:

  1. Visit one of the missions in Peoria. Ask for a tour and a chance to talk to a staff person. Call ahead.
  2. Make a shopping trip to a grocery store on Peoria's south side. Record your findings.

3. Find out how to provide food for a foreign child through World Vision.
4. Research the needs of citizens of Marshall County who live below the poverty line.
5. Devise a project of your own.

Practicing the Presence

I. **Definition**

The experiential recognition of God's presence and care, at any given moment of our existence, as acknowledged by word or thought.

II. **Scriptural Support**

A. Psalm 139:7–10

B. Psalm 27:7–8

C. Psalm 63:1–3, 6–8

D. 1 Thessalonians 5:17

III. **Insights From Spiritual Leaders**

A. "There is no mode of life in the world more pleasing and more full of delight than continual conversation with God; only those who practice and experience it can understand it. I do not, however, advise you to pursue it for this purpose. We should not be seeking consolation from this practice, but let us do it motivated by love and because God wishes it. . . . I cannot understand how religious people can live contented lives without the practice of the presence of God. For myself I withdraw as much as I can to the deepest recesses of my soul with Him, and while I am thus with Him I fear nothing; but the least turning away from Him is hell for me. . . . Do not be discouraged by the resistance you will encounter from your human nature; you must go against your human inclination. Often, in the beginning, you will think that you are wasting time, but you must go on, be determined and persevere in it until death, despite all the difficulties" (Brother Lawrence, *The Practice of the Presence of God*, p. 60–62).

B. God dwells in His creation and is everywhere indivisibly present in all His works. This is boldly taught by prophet and apostle, and is accepted by Christian theology generally. That is, it appears in the books, but for some reason it has not sunk into the average Christian's heart so as to become a part of his believing self. . . . The Presence and the manifestation of the Presence are not the same. There can be the one without the other. God is here when we are wholly unaware of it. He is manifest only when and as we are aware of His presence. On our part, there must be surrender to the Spirit of God, for His work is to show us the Father and the Son. If we cooperate with Him in loving obedience, God will manifest Himself to us, and that manifestation will be the difference between a nominal Christian life and a life radiant with the light of His face" (A. W. Tozer, *The Pursuit of God*, p. 61, 64).

C. "Early on, Puritans perfected methods of meditation and contemplation supportive of heart religion. According to the master guide of Puritan contemplation, Richard Baxter, contemplation should occur at stated times to avoid omission, frequently to prevent shyness between God and the soul and prevent unskillfulness and 'loss of heat and life,' and seasonably. Prayer should be engaged in several times daily, more frequently on the sabbath, on special occasions when God warms the heart, when sick, and when dying. Devout Puritans often spent entire days in prayer. They frequently threw up 'ejaculatory' prayers as occasion demanded. Obviously the goal was to 'pray without ceasing1 (1 Thess 5:17)" (E. Glenn Hinson, "Puritan Spirituality" in *Protestant Spiritual Traditions*, p. 172–173).

D. "With Christ at the center of your life you can help your child begin to focus his life on Christ. A spiritually healthy home has a God-consciousness about it—that is, every member is aware that Christ is present minute by minute and involved in what the family is doing. You can foster God-consciousness by praying and praising God together throughout the day, not just at mealtimes or bedtime. Talk with your child about the beauty of God's creation as you drive through the country. When you see people who are needy, talk about the ways you can help them just as Jesus helped others. In these ways you will help your child see that loving Christ is more than just something you do on Sunday" (Neil Anderson and Steve Russo, *The Seduction of Our Children*, p. 187).

IV. Practical Tips

A. Think of the members of the Trinity as ever present, of yourself as never alone.

B. Think of every action as something not only done for God, but with God.

C. Verbalize the truth. Speak to Jesus as if He really is with you in the car, in the kitchen, on the job, etc.

D. Express your pleasure to the members of the Godhead that they are with you. Tell them that you enjoy them and love them.

V. Assignment

A. Practice the presence at work, at home, at play, etc.

B. Record your experience on your Spiritual Disciplines Personal Experience Record.

Confession

I. Definition

The practice of admitting, primarily to God and secondarily to people, that our specified thoughts and actions are sin.

II. Scriptural Support

A. 1 John 1:8–10

B. James 5:16

C. Acts 19:14–19

D. Psalm 32:1–5

III. Insight From Spiritual Leaders

A. "The intuitive realization that, as sinners, we are rightly objects of God's wrath is the immediate cause of flight from God. When we sense that God is near, then, like Peter, we sense our moral misshapenness, realize our shortcomings, and remember our many acts of willful rebellion. The sudden vision of our God can fill us, as it did Peter, with fear and impel us to run and try to hide. This impulse is perhaps our first reaction when we discover some specific sin in our lives. . . . Then John tells us that we are to deal with the reality of who God is, not just the reality of who we are. God is forgiving and loves us completely. Fixing our eyes on God, we are to reject Adam's remedy of flight and, against all our instincts, are to come to God rather than cringe away" (Lawrence Richards, *A Practical Theology of Spirituality*, p. 125, 129–130).

B. "Spiritual discipline calls for a regular acknowledgment of our true nature and the specific acts and attitudes of the recent past that have not been pleasurable to God as he has sought our fellowship and our obedience. . . . When I first began to follow Christ seriously, He pointed out many major behavior and attitude patterns that, like boulders, had to be removed. And as the years went by, many of those great big boulders did indeed got removed. But when they began to disappear, I discovered a whole new layer of action and attitude in my life that I had not previously seen. But Christ saw them and rebuked them one by one. The removal process began again. Then I reached that point in my Christian life where Christ and I were dealing with stones and pebbles. They are too numerous to imagine, and as far as I can see, for the rest of my days on earth I will be working with the many stones and pebbles in my life. Every day at spiritual discipline time, there is likely to be a new stab at the clearing process" (Gordon MacDonald, *Ordering Your Private World*, p. 152–13).

C. "Confession is a difficult Discipline for us because we all too often view the believing community as a fellowship of saints before we see it as a fellowship of sinners. We feel that everyone else has advanced so far into holiness that we are isolated and alone in our sin. We cannot bear to reveal our failures and shortcomings to others. We imagine that we are the only ones who have not stepped onto the high road to heaven. Therefore, we hide ourselves from one another and live in veiled lies and hypocrisy" (Richard Foster, *Celebration of Discipline*, p. 145).

IV. Practical Tips

A. Be receptive to the conviction of the Holy Spirit as you read the Bible.

B. Do not be overly introspective

C. When you confess to a person you have sinned against, do not make excuses.

V. Assignment

A. Each time you have a devotional period, ask God to reveal your sins.

B. Ask a trusted friend to pray for any besetting sin.

C. Record your experience on your Personal Experience Record.

Personal and Intercessory Prayer

I. Definition

The practice of approaching God, on behalf of ourselves and others, that He might meet the expressed needs.

II. Scriptural Support

A. The invitation to pray

1. John 16:24
2. Hebrews 4:14–16

B. Conditions for answered prayer

1. 1 John 3:22–23
2. 1 John 5:14–15

C. The subjects of prayer

1. Philippians 4:6–7
2. 1 Timothy 2:1–2

III. Insights From Spiritual Leaders

A. "The power of prayer is nowhere more clearly manifest than in the intercessions of the faithful. Through the prayers of the church, people are healed, lives are transformed, nations are changed. . . . Intercession not only powerfully aids our fellow human beings, but it also revitalizes the spiritual life of the intercessor. . . . It is important to remember that the intercessory prayer of many humble people nurtured in the churches of evangelical Pietism has been responsible for the great missionary outreach of Protestantism" (Donald Bloesch, *The Struggle of Prayer*, p. 87–89).

B. "Quite frankly, I could not get on at all without a prayer list, not only because it tames my wandering mind, but also because it insures that I will not neglect things that are important to me, including the many requests for personal prayer which I receive. In addition, a prayer list is perfect for keeping track of answers to prayer. . . . If you do not have a prayer list, start small. Simply list the relationship and matters most important to you on a 3x5 card, add a few specifics under the names, and put it in your wallet for daily reference. I guarantee that if you use it, it will greatly enhance your prayer life" (R. Kent Hughes, *Disciplines of a Godly Man*, p. 100).

C. "I realize that to say prayer is expected of us may make the children of a nonconformist, anti-authoritarian age bristle a bit. Those who have been brought up under the authority of Christ and the Bible, however, know that the will of God is for us to pray. But we also believe His will is good. . . . There is a sense in which prayer needs to be taught to a child of God no more than a baby needs to be taught to cry. But crying for basic needs is minimal communication, and we must soon grow beyond that infancy. The Bible says we must pray for the glory of God, in His will, in faith, in the name of Jesus, with persistence, and more. A child of God gradually learns to pray like this in the same way that a growing child learns to talk. To pray as expected, to pray as a maturing Christian, and to pray effectively, we must say with the disciples, in Luke 11:1, 'Lord, teach us to pray' " (Donald Whitney, *Spiritual Disciplines For The Christian Life*, p. 62–63, 66).

IV. Practical Tips

A. During devotional times, ask God to lead you to pray for what you should.

B. Keep some sort of list to pray from.

C. Keep a list of answers, especially of personal requests God has answered for you.

V. Assignment

A. Pray through your church directory, two families at a time, during your devotional periods.

B. Keep a list of answered prayers between now and the end of the class.

C. Record your finding in the Spiritual Disciplines Record.

Celebration

I. Definition

The practice of deliberately enjoying God and his blessings, being certain to praise Him for all aspects of our lives, while cultivating a carefree and joyous spirit.

II. Scriptural Support

A. Ecclesiastes 9:7–9

B. Nehemiah 8:8–12

C. Psalms 146:1–2; 150:1–6

D. Proverbs 17:22

E. Philippians 4:4

F. 1 Thessalonians 5:16–18

III. Insight From Spiritual Leaders

A. "Far and away the most important benefit of celebration is that it saves us from taking ourselves too seriously. This is a desperately needed grace for all those who are earnest about the Spiritual Disciplines. It is an occupational hazard of devout folk to become stuffy bores. This should not be. Of all people, we should be the most free, alive, interesting. Celebration adds a note of gaiety, festivity, hilarity to our lives. After all, Jesus rejoiced so fully in life that he was accused of being a winebibber and a glutton. Many of us lead such sour lives that we cannot possibly be accused of such things"(*Richard Foster, Celebration of Discipline*, p. 196).

B. "That is, praise should go to God from His people simply because He is God. We are to praise God for who He is and for what He does. In the midst of our deepest distress we do not need to thank the Lord for the hurt, but we must praise the Lord because he is still our God" (Ronald B. Allen, *Praise*, p. 3).

C. "In prayers of praise, we are unabashed, often unrestrained in praising God for what he is and for what he does. Now, not every Christian finds it easy to offer prayers of praise, and it may be that the extent to which we do spontaneously praise God is one of the marks of growth in the spiritual life. Practically speaking, one of the ways to grow spiritually is to go through the motions, to mouth the words of praise even when we do not have the feeling. The feelings will follow the motions" (Sylvia Fleming Crocker, "Prayer as a Model of Communication," p. 873).

IV. **Practical Tips**

A. Meditate on passages that encourage praise and enjoyment of life.

B. If you are too serious, ask God to help you mature into a more balanced person.

V. **Assignment**

A. Sing to the Lord each time you meet with him for a devotional time.

B. Examine your general attitude toward the Christian life. What, if anything, does this discipline do to modify it?

C. Record finding in your Spiritual Disciplines, Record.

Appendix D

Final Summary and Sharing

I. **Review of the Spiritual Disciplines**

    A. The Disciplines of Reflection

        1. Solitude
        2. Silence
        3. Journaling

    B. The Discipline of Fasting

    C. The Disciplines of Bible Study

        1. Bible Intake
        2. Devotional Bible Study
        3. The Use of Imagination in Bible Study

    D. The Discipline of Simplicity

    E. The Disciplines of Prayer

        1. Practicing the Presence
        2. Confession
        3. Personal and Intercessory Prayer
        4. Celebration

II. **The Need to Persevere in Spiritual Disciplines**

    A. "Even with the consistent evaluation of priorities, the Godly person will continue to be a busy person. However, the busy person is also the one most tempted to lapse in the practice of the very Disciplines that lead to Godliness. Without practicing the Spiritual Disciplines we will not be Godly, but neither will we be Godly without perseverance in practicing the Disciplines. Even a slow, plodding perseverance in the Spiritual Disciplines is better than a sometimes spectacular but generally inconsistent practice" (Donald Whitney, *Spiritual Disciplines for the Christian Life*, p. 227).

    B. "The key to my ability was repetition. I practiced and practiced and practiced again. I gave the sport my total commitment.

I tried everything I could in every way I could to perfect my skills. It was like an obsession. It paid off for me as a player. I'm not so sure in life. If I had given that same devotion then to my faith, which is what I do now, I'd have been a better person in the long run" (Pete Maravich, *USA Today*, 18 January, 1988).

III. Potential Benefits and Potential Dangers of the Spiritual Disciplines

A. Potential Benefits

1. Spirituality of the Heart
2. Production of Spiritual Fruit
3. Variety for the Devotional Life
4. A Directed Approach to Spiritual Growth
5. Psychological Health
6. Improved Corporate Worship

B. Potential Dangers

1. Subjectivity

2. Convergence with Unorthodox Movements
   a. Asceticism
   b. Catholicism
   c. Eastern Mysticism
   d. The New Age Movement
   e. Quietism

3. Legalism

4. Pride

5. Privitization

IV. Assignment

A. Practice the disciplines for four more weeks independently.

B. Complete your Spiritual Disciplines Record.

C. Complete the Spiritual Well-being Scale for the third time.

D. Give your record and well-being test directly to Dan.

Appendix E

Literature Related
to the Spiritual Disciplines

This chapter will survey many of the best sources for the study of the classical spiritual disciplines. Its purpose is to expose the reader to the literature of the field, and to lay groundwork for a theology of the disciplines. The sources surveyed will appear under three major headings: general spirituality, combined disciplines, and particular disciplines. Within these major categories, articles follow books, and works appear in order of my perception of their comparative value.

General Spirituality

The books and periodicals reviewed in this section survey various topics within the field of spirituality. While not dealing specifically with spiritual disciplines, they share a common field with them.

The Study of Spirituality (Jones, Wainwright, and Yarnold 1986) is a comprehensive work deserving serious attention. Its three major sections deal with the theology of spirituality, the history of spirituality, and pastoral spirituality. The latter section is practical and thought-provoking from the perspective of parish ministry. Bibliographic material at the head of every subsection is valuable. The book suffers at times from the sacramentalism of some of its contributors.

A Practical Theology of Spirituality begins with an excellent section that yields the definition of spirituality as "having to do with being an integrated person in the fullest sense" (Richards 1987, 11). The crux of the book, found in its second part, deals with spiritual development. It addresses the issues of identity, intimacy, sinfulness, lordship, mortality, holiness, and commitment. A short chapter entitled "Prayer of the Heart" deals with several aspects of prayer life. Richards's balanced approach to the subject distinguishes this contribution.

Dynamics of Spiritual Life: An Evangelical Theology of Renewal (Lovelace 1988) is several hundred pages in length and deals with basic elements of spiritual renewal. This term, not to be confused with revivalism, has to do with regained spiritual vigor. The Holy Spirit's work within is seen as the primary source of individual renewal. Congregational renewal, according to Lovelace, comes from preaching, teaching, and house-to-house counsel.

Spiritual Depression: Its Causes and Cure (Lloyd-Jones 1965) is a compilation of sermons. It presents biblical perspectives on issues such as feelings, tiredness, trials, and chastening. An excellent chapter, entitled "That One Sin," affirms that every sin is forgivable. This book demonstrates that Scripture is sufficient.

Psychotherapy and the Spiritual Quest (Benner 1981) is an attempt to integrate psychology and the theology of spirituality. He argues for "the legitimacy of calling psychotherapy a religious or spiritual process" (Benner 1988, 13). His chapter on Christian spirituality helps the reader understand how different spiritual traditions fit on the spectrum of objective to subjective authority and how psychological dynamics affect each. Numerous case studies are used as a basis of showing how psychological and spiritual needs cannot be neatly separated. One disturbing aspect of the book is Banner's apparent hesitation to confront his clients with the gospel.

In Protestant Spiritual Traditions (Senn 1986), spirituality is defined as the way in which one's relationship with God is conceived and expressed. This process is examined as understood in Lutheran, Reformed, Anabaptist, Anglican, Puritan, and Methodist traditions. This book can enhance appreciation for approaches different than one's own.

Five Views on Sanctification (Dieter and others 1987) presents models for Christian growth from Wesleyan, Reformed, Pentecostal, Keswick, and Augustinian-Dispensational perspectives, respectively. Each article is accompanied by irenic responses from those who disagree with certain aspects of it.

The Westminster Dictionary of Christian Spirituality (Wakefield 1983) includes approximately three hundred twenty-five articles, fifty-seven by its editor Gordon Wakefield. High-quality entries cover a broad spectrum of authors, works, persons, subjects, and virtues. However, its admittedly ecumenical viewpoint allows it to view uncritically false religions, such as Taoism, and heretical practices, such as prayer for the dead.

The Crisis of Piety: Essays Toward a Theology of the Christian Life (Bloesch 1988) is a valuable commentary on the need for modern-day spiritual renewal. Bloesch contends that devotion must yield service to

Christ, not simply worship. While rejecting liberal theology, he prods conservatives to responsible social action. An excellent chapter on devotional life highlights potential benefits and dangers of spiritual disciplines.

In *The Pursuit of God* (Tozer 1982), the author insists on biblical foundations, yet is equally insistent that Scripture must be taught and understood so as to affect the inner man. Tozer (1982, 9) says of teachers that "too many of these seem satisfied to teach the fundamentals of faith year after year, strangely unaware that there is, in their ministry, no manifest Presence, nor anything unusual in their personal lives." This book helps the believer experience the God of the Bible.

In *True Spirituality* (Schaeffer 1971) the writer contends that the historic facts of Christ's death and resurrection should affect the believer in the here and now. A relationship with the Savior, he says, should bring peace with God, self, and fellow-humans. This, in addition, implies intimacy with God, psychological wholeness, and social responsibility. For Schaeffer (1971, 180) "true spirituality—The Christian life—flows on into the total culture."

The Essence of Spiritual Religion (Trueblood 1936) urges a breaking down of any dichotomy between one's "secular" and "religious" life. As a result of deep inner life, daily work should be a ministry. The author is highly critical of the legalism and ceremonialism of the Roman Catholic faith, advocating, instead, the priesthood of believers. A weakness of the work is the author's undue optimism concerning men's eagerness to respond to spiritual truth.

Spirituality Through the Centuries: Ascetics and Mystics of the Western Church (Walsh n.d.) is a collection of analyses of spiritual writers, from the third through seventeenth centuries. While it is a helpful survey, it contains more analysis of the writings than exposure to the writings themselves.

Christian Spirituality: The Essential Guide to the Most Influential Spiritual Writings of the Christian Tradition (Magill and McGreal 1988) is immensely valuable, surveying a wide range of writers whose contributions span from the second century through the twentieth century. One major work of each author is considered, often with parts the text itself present. Each entry is accompanied by a short biographical sketch of the author, and a summary of the major themes of his or her work. The work manifests diversity in the theological persuasions of both the authors and their reviewers. It is an unparalleled introduction to spiritual writings.

Pascal's *Pensees* (Pascal 1958) is a collection of sayings, and short essays, as well as commentary on Scripture, by a French scientific and mathematical genius. The book shows that, as is proper, the author was drawn closer to

God by diligent study of the universe and its order. It is a model integration of faith and science.

Benedicta Ward translated *The Sayings of the Desert Fathers* (1975). It is a collection of short statements by men who lived in the deserts of Egypt during the third through fifth centuries, A. D. The solitary life of these individuals produced deep insight into the life of prayer. This work also shows that, in the breaking of solitude, there is love to be shared in the service of others. The writings, at times, exhibit extreme asceticism and pride.

In *The New Man* (Merton 1961) the author sets forth what he sees as essential elements of the spiritual life. Our spiritual growth is seen as depending on union with the Holy Spirit, and the realization of love, received from God, and given to other men. Christian life is not merely an imitation of Christ but a dependency on Christ to live through us. This book is marred by its teaching that water baptism unites the believer with Christ.

The Fight (White 1976) faces the fact that the Christian life is often a struggle. It warns the believer to beware of Satan, and his host. Prayer (at set times, and by practicing the presence), as well as regular Bible study, is set forth as essential to victory. Other helpful chapters deal with holiness of character and divine guidance. Summaries and practical assignments conclude most sections.

The Contemplative Pastor (Peterson 1989) challenges the normally hectic pace of the American clergyman. It urges pastors to take charge of their schedules, so as to devote time to three most important things: preaching, prayer, and listening. He urges that a program orientation be avoided. Instead, patient, enduring, personal work with people is encouraged. Pastoral spirituality also means being willing to engage in small talk for the sake of an opening from God for ministry. Peterson might have mentioned that it may take time, struggle, and patience to get some congregations to accept a contemplative pastor.

Knowing God (Packer 1973) was written to help people know the God of the Bible through his attributes, and to also realize the practical implications of a relationship with him through Jesus Christ. Packer makes it clear that a person can know a great deal about God and godliness, without knowing him well personally. The reader is then invited to know God through such attributes as his majesty, wisdom, veracity, grace, and wrath. Finally, the believer is shown his privileges in relationship to the Father: sonship, guidance, and help during trials.

Intimacy With God (Booker 1983) also invites the reader to know God through his attributes. A great strength of the book is that it expresses the attributes in simple terms rather than in formal theological ones. Each attribute is linked to a hypothetical, practical question. The chapters are completed with review questions. An appendix provides extensive scriptural support for each of nine characteristics of God that Booker covers.

Mysticism: An Evangelical Option? (Corduan 1991) provides philosophical groundwork for the study of mysticism, from a Christian viewpoint, by asking whether one can be an evangelical believer and find value in it. While recognizing that all mysticism has common concepts such as worship, prayer, and bliss, he recognizes Christian mysticism, grounded in the Word of God, as superior. While rejecting the idea of valid Christian revelation or experience apart from Scripture, Corduan defends the idea of experiencing Christian truth through the Holy Spirit and mystical communion with Christ.

Faith Misguided: Exposing the Dangers of Mysticism (Johnson 1988) is a rigorous critique of mysticism within Christian circles. The writer strongly criticizes believers who give authority to their religious experiences. He is right to be concerned about the lack of proper theological foundation manifested, at times, by Watchman Nee, and some charismatic Christians. His objections, however, may be unbalanced. He seems to explain away Paul's experience in Acts 9 where he is clearly said to have understood what others did not. It should also be noted that, while experience does not validate Scripture, Scripture is to be experienced. Dead orthodoxy is the alternative. Finally, the division of his bibliography into "pro-mysticism" and "anti-mysticism" literature is simplistic.

Mysticism: A Study in the Nature and Development of Man's Spiritual Consciousness (Underhill 1940) stands as a classic presentation of Christian mysticism. The author urges a vital experiential life with God. Her work, though, is often extreme as she invites the reader onto the "mystic way," and to lose himself in the "reality."

Christian Mysticism: The Future of a Tradition (Egan 1984) examines Christian mysticism theologically, biblically, and historically. The majority of the book is given to the works of Roman Catholic writers such as Teresa of Avila, John of the Cross, and Thomas Merton. Common themes are self-surrender, centering on God, and love for others. It also includes an attempt to define mysticism. The book suffers from theological narrowness and lack of biblical epistomolgy.

"The Power and the Presence" by Hayford and others appeared in *Leadership* (1991). It is a discussion of the supernatural experiences of men of various theological persuasions. The interaction is candid and unapologetic. The article also includes a section on spiritual warfare.

"Evangelical Spirituality: A Church Historian's Perspective" (Lovelace 1988) was published in *The Journal of the Evangelical Theological Society*. It bemoans the fact that spirituality has been a neglected dimension of scholarly study. Calling to mind the historic spirituality of the church, the author urges modern believers to be renewed through a recognition of God's holiness and human depravity. He also suggests that more attention be given to spiritual disciplines and that discipleship challenges need to be more rigorous.

A companion article in *The Journal of the Evangelical Theological Society* is "Evangelical Spirituality: A Biblical Scholar's Perspective" (Waltke 1988). Spirituality, Waltke says, has to do with loving God through faith in him, fear of him, and repentance before him. It also includes love of men and total care of them, although not necessarily through the structures of human government. While not opening the door for irresponsibility, the author recognizes that the church's ultimate social destiny will not be reached this side of heaven.

"Growth: An Act of the Will?" (Petersen 1988) ran in *Leadership*. It is a reflection on the interplay of God's will and ours. The phrase "willed passivity" integrates the two in Petersen's estimation. This does not imply spiritual sloth. Rather, it suggests that God, through events and other people, brings most of life to us. Willed passivity is an attentiveness to God as he works.

"Type B Spirituality" (Felker 1988) is a refreshing article that appeared in *Leadership*. It is the author's admission that devotional life is difficult for him and that, at times, he feels like a failure. He sees diversity during devotional times as a help. He also uses regularity of time with God, ministry faithfulness, marriage quality, and victory over besetting sins, as measures of his spiritual growth.

"Recovering the Heart of Christian Spirituality" (Demarest and Raup 1989) appeared in the *Criswell Theological Review*. It seeks to show that theological and biblical study should go hand-in-hand with piety. The authors blame an illegitimate dichotomy between dogmatic and mystical theology, emotionalism, intellectualism, and moralism for the present failure to integrate serious study with fervent devotion. Such heart intimacy with God, they say, can be developed through quiet listening and fervent prayer.

J. I. Packer wrote "An Introduction to Systematic Spirituality" (1991) in *Crux* to encourage the healthy allegiance of theological studies and spirituality. He argues for a study of theology that is first exegetical, relying on a disciplined approach to Scripture. But this must be followed with a synthesis that includes "the relational activity of trusting, loving, worshipping, obeying, sewing, and glorifying God" (Packer 1990, 6). Thus he argues for the study of theology itself as a devotional discipline.

"Hermeneutics and the Spiritual Life" (Waltke 1987) appeared in *Crux*. It calls attention to the fact that dependence on the Holy Spirit, in the exegetical process, is increasingly overlooked. Through extensive reference to modern works on hermeneutics, Waltke demonstrates a departure from the spiritual emphasis of the Reformation. He makes his point well: those who seek to teach exegesis, that is divorced from vibrant spirituality, fail.

"Evangelicals and Spirituality" (Hingley 1990) appeared in *Themelios* and expresses concern over certain contemporary spiritual practices, particularly in the area of spiritual disciplines. While recognizing the value of disciplines, Hingley cautions that they do not guarantee intimacy with God. He also warns against employing Eastern forms that may hurt the spiritual progress of new converts from Transcendental Meditation and similar movements. Other potential dangers listed are legalism and the undisciplined use of imagination.

"Lost in the Mystical Myths" (Bloesch 1991) is an excellent *Christianity Today* article, warning against potential excesses in classical mysticism and modern, sometimes pluralistic, spirituality. Bloesch differentiates between the new spirituality, classical mysticism, and biblical or evangelical spirituality. He calls the believer back to the Bible as a base for developing religious affections.

Combined Disciplines

The group of works below each deal with several spiritual disciplines in various combinations. They are often especially convenient to use and help in the integration of the many disciplines.

Perhaps the single most beneficial combined work is *The Spirit of the Disciplines: Understanding How God Changes Lives* (Willard 1988). It provides the sort of extensive theological reflection in which the practice of specific disciplines is properly grounded. Of the failure to properly emphasize personal devotion to God, in the context of ministry, he says:

> The American church has overestimated the good that comes from mere scientific progress or doctrinal correctness, or from social progress, missionary work, and evangelism. . . . And as a result, the church at present has lost any realistic and specific sense of what it means for the individual believer to "grow in the grace and knowledge of our Lord and Savior Jesus Christ," as 2 Peter 3:18 expresses

it. In fact, it has lost sight of the type of life in which such growth would be a realistic and predictable possibility (Willard 1988, 16).

Willard's solution to this problem is the practice of various spiritual disciplines with a view to service as a practical outworking of such devotion. He deals with fourteen disciplines, evenly balanced between what he calls "disciplines of abstinence" and "disciplines of engagement." His sections on fasting, secrecy, and celebration are exceptionally good. In a chapter entitled "Spiritual Life: The Body's Fulfillment," he presents a most insightful model for the integration of the body into the concept of Christian spirituality. He thus provides a safeguard against such extremes as asceticism and pagan mysticism. This work also contains a fine section on the easy yoke and what the author perceives as the ultimate value of the disciplines: to help the believer live a life like Christ lived, by engaging in the spiritual practices he engaged in.

Celebration of Discipline: The Path to Spiritual Growth (Foster 1988) deserves notice as the work that revived, among Evangelicals, a now burgeoning interest in classical disciplines. Foster states that: "If we ever expect to grow in grace, we must pay the price of a consciously chosen course of action which involves both individual and group life" (Foster 1978, 8). For the promotion of group life, he presents confession, worship, celebration, and guidance. The last term refers to seeking God's direction as a community of believers. This book is the product of extensive research and serves as a good introduction to other spiritual resources. It is full of spiritual insight and practical advice worth following. Nevertheless, it is sometimes theologically suspect. The author is heavily influenced by Quaker sources that seem to lead him, occasionally, away from the bedrock of Scripture in search of "inner light."

Another valuable contribution by Foster is *Meditative Prayer* (1983). This booklet combines silence (listening), practicing the presence, and the use of imagination under the umbrella of meditation. Surrender, confession, and acceptance of God's ways with us are seen as necessary to the process.

Spiritual Disciplines for the Christian Life (Whitney 1991) draws heavily on Puritan and Evangelical writers in producing an outstanding contribution to the field. The theme of the book, discipline for godliness, is taken from 1 Tim 4:7. Its first chapter sets forth a concise biblical theology of the practices it advocates. Two more chapters urge extensive study of Scripture. This emphasis on objective grounding of devotional practices in the Word of God should engender the trust of the Biblicist. The chapter on serving is a good challenge to action. The final portion of the book is a frank and encouraging recognition that the cultivation of the spiritual life requires continual, rigorous, attention.

Disciplines of a Godly Man (Hughes 1991) was written for a male audience. The author points out that women are generally much more spiritual than men in American culture, and challenges male readers to mature. While he urges the practice of prayer, confession, meditation, and worship, these classical disciplines are not his whole emphasis. His main thrust is to call men to live in integrity with others. Insightful chapters are included on marriage, fatherhood, and friendship, as well as leadership, giving, and ministry. The presentation of these under the paradigm of disciplines is very helpful. His approach is fresh and effective in protecting the reader from undue inwardness. While the tone of the book may be criticized as occasionally harsh, it may equally be recognized as a straightforward challenge to wayward men.

Ordering Your Private World (MacDonald 1984) urges undisciplined persons to begin using their time in eternally significant ways. The writer sees drivenness as a prime motivator for misuse of time, and a sense of God's call as its antidote. His analysis is worthy of note:

> To order my life according to the expectations of myself and others;
> and to value myself according to the opinion of others; these can play
> havoc with my inner world. But to operate on the basis of God's call
> is to enjoy a great deal of order within. (MacDonald 1985, 61)

MacDonald's section on difficulties in prayer is helpful. He lists the unnaturalness of prayer, our lack of willingness to admit need, and lack of prayer answers as common discouragements. The chapter on the need for physical rest for spiritual advancement challenges busyness. One weakness in this book is the author's habit of quoting secondary sources without benefit of the original contexts.

Dependence on the Holy Spirit, and service to others flowing from a rich inner life, are the major emphases of *Moving in the Spirit: Becoming a Contemplative in Action* (Hauser 1986). These are developed with great practical insight. Each chapter concludes with helpful questions for reflection. Hauser's chapter on journaling gives workable suggestions for making and reviewing entries. The reader should be aware that the author's Jesuit belief in the fundamental trustworthiness of human nature (Hauser 1986, 2), may cause him to place too much trust in his thoughts.

Calvin Miller (1984) is the author of *The Table of Inwardness*. He suggests that one is drawn into deeper intimacy with Christ through such practices as silence, simplicity, obedience, and the use of imagination.

Four potential impediments to such intimacy are noted and discussed: sex, food, power, and hurriedness. Yet Miller does not promote asceticism or exalt poverty. He makes it clear that purity of intent is central to a rich spiritual life.

Holy Living (Taylor 1988) was written in 1650 and stands today as a classic in devotional practice. The author advocates traditional disciplines such as practicing the presence, fasting, Bible reading, and prayer. To these he adds helpful material on modesty, obedience to authority, and purity of intention. With regard to the latter, he stresses that "he is to be called evil who is good for his own sake" (Taylor 1988, 19). This entire piece is characterized by an earnest zeal. It may be noted, however, that this zeal becomes imbalanced in places, to the extent that legalism seems to snuff out joy.

The Imitation of Christ (Kempis 1984) stands as one of the most widely read devotional books in the history of the church. Divided into four "books" and over one hundred chapters it is ideal for short meditations. Hundreds of scriptural quotations or illusions are present in the text. Deep insight into many spiritual arenas is present. Of Scripture reading the author says: "If thou wouldst profit by thy reading, read humbly, simply, honestly, and not desiring to win a character for learning" (Kempis 1984, 15). Other helpful sections address economy of words, appreciation of adversity, silence, solitude, and inward life. While not overshadowing its benefits, it should be noted that this work is sometimes morose, legalistic, and even disrespectful of man's God-given dignity.

A Serious Call to a Devout and Holy Life (Law 1966) was written by the eighteenth century high Churchman William Law. It has strongly impacted not only those of his own school, but pietists and Evangelicals as well. Two chapters are given to demonstrate how the rich may temper their lifestyles and use their assets to help others. These are presented under the example of Miranda, a matron of the author's acquaintance. Several chapters are given to various forms of prayer. Another presents helpful suggestions for devotional use of Psalms. An unusually high regard for the intelligence of women, for the era, as well as concern for their education, is exhibited in a chapter entitled, "female education."

A Testament of Devotion (1941) was written by Thomas Kelly. Early chapters urge practicing the presence, inward quietness, and holy obedience. Concerning the latter, Kelly writes against "half-way" commitment, taking to task various fellowships, including his own Quaker constituency. In a chapter entitled "The Eternal Now and Social Concern," the relationship between contemplation and social action is discussed. The reader is warned not to be compelled by social concerns to the extent that contemplation of the eternal is neglected. While gaining from this book, many readers will still feel uncomfortable with its intense focus on inner light and experience.

Working the Angles: The Shape of Pastoral Integrity (Peterson 1987) is written from a pastor's perspective but can benefit laypersons as well. It is concerned with the disciplines of prayer, Scripture study, and spiritual direction. To facilitate a strong prayer life Peterson urges a "Sabbath" during which there is time for quiet contemplation, enjoyment of nature, and meditative reading of Psalms. His emphasis on meditation, as an integral part of the exegetical process, is welcome.

Sadhana: A Way to God (de Mello 1984) presents Christian spiritual exercises in forms normally associated with Eastern religions. Disciplines such as meditation, prayer, silence, and the use of imagination in Bible study are addressed. Detailed instruction in bodily relaxation, for engagement in these disciplines, is given. While much of the material is helpful, caution is in order. This work is sometimes too subjective and leaves the imagination ungrounded. It is definitely not for new believers.

Particular Disciplines

The titles that appear in this section of the chapter represent extensive work in specific disciplines, or in a limited number of closely-related disciplines. Among these are silence, solitude, journaling, fasting, Bible study, simplicity, practicing the presence, confession, petition, and celebration.

Silence/Solitude

While not synonymous, silence and solitude are closely related in literature and practice and are thus treated together here.

The Way of the Heart (Nouwen 1981b) is given to the disciplines of silence, solitude, and prayer, as developed against the backdrop of the desert fathers of the third and fourth centuries, A. D. Nouwen's own words best summarize the book:

> My first task is to explore what it means for us to flee from the world. This raises the question of solitude. My second task is to define silence as an essential element of a spirituality of ministry. Finally, I want to challenge you with the vocation to pray always. (Nouwen 19 81, 4)

Nouwen calls pastors to forsake their worldliness and busyness for regular periods of solitude. He also extols silence for its benefits to preaching, counseling, and organizing.

Making All Things New: An Invitation to the Spiritual Life (Nouwen 1981a) was written to address such hazards to the spiritual life as busyness, discontent, and worry. The last problem is Nouwen's main focus. After examining several passages of Scripture orienting believers to kingdom priorities, the author finds the cure for worry in solitude. Through this discipline, the believer realizes that discontent rages within. Through it, also, he gradually comes into contact with God at a more intimate level, being thus relieved of his fears.

The Other Side of Silence: A Guide to Christian Meditation (Kelsey 1976) sees periods of solitude and silence as fundamental to closeness with God. Solid scriptural support is offered for the practices. Many readers, however, will be uncomfortable with the amount of discussion given to breathing techniques, disengagement of the analytical thought processes, and the use of images.

"Getting to Know God" (Kroll 1991) was published in *Prokope*. It was written to help busy pastors realize the need to be alone and quiet. Acknowledging the pastor's many responsibilities, Kroll urges the clergy to make these practices a priority. The back porch under the stars, the country, a stream, or even a bed are suggested as places to encounter God in silence.

"One Minute Maturity" (Ortberg 1991) was written for *Leadership*. It affirms that there is no such thing. Commitment and change, Ortberg says, will be required. Arriving early at work and scheduling retreat days are encouraged for solitude. Silence can be enjoyed by scheduling time in which not to talk or turn on a radio. Helpful insights on confession and fasting further enhance the value of this article.

"A Time to Keep Silence" (Moskal 1990) was published in *Industry Week*. Its uniqueness lies in the fact that it shows the appreciation of secular businesses for silence. They have found it to clarify thought, focus attention, and increase confidence. This should help believers appreciate the psychological benefits that may accompany the spiritual ones they so enjoy.

"Let Us Dare to Have Solitude" (Tillich 1957) appeared in the *Quarterly Review* and asserts that one can have relief from loneliness and alienation from other people through solitude. The author distinguishes loneliness and solitude as follows:

> The wisdom of our language has grasped these two sides of man's being alone. It has created the word loneliness in order to emphasize the pain of being alone, and it has created the word solitude in order to emphasize the glory of being alone. (Tillich 1957, 10–11)

He says that what a man does with solitude is his religion. From solitary contact with God, a man encounters himself, asks questions concerning societal justice, and enhances his creativity. He is thus ready to impact other men in meaningful ways, and to relieve his loneliness, and theirs.

Julie Hubbard-McNall authored "Breaking Free: The Experience of Solitude" (1991) for the *American Baptist Quarterly*. Her thesis is that solitude, practiced regularly by every person, could change the world. She argues that quiet reflection allows one to appreciate his own uniqueness and thus that of others, making acceptance of differences easier. It also is seen as a seed bed for vision of a better society.

In "Healing Through Solitude and Community," (Cornwall 1981) the writer stresses the value of both solitude and fellowship in mental healing. In her own words, "solitude is needed for introspection and prayer for sorting things out in one's mind, but without human encounter and interaction one may distort the experience" (Cornwall 1981, 77). This *Quarterly Review* article puts its strongest emphasis on community and thus protects against the abuse of solitude.

"Silence as Creative Therapy: A Contemplative Approach to Pastoral Care" (Morgan 1975) was contributed to the *Journal of Pastoral Care*. Morgan notes that silence has no intrinsic value. Rather it should be viewed as a medium to encounter with God. This fact should lead the pastoral counselor to value silence as well as the use of the right word at the right time. The author's main point is that once God has begun to minister in silence, he will continue through the words of the pastor.

Journaling

Journaling: A Spirit Journey (Broyles 1988) was written as an introduction to the subject. Broyles is careful to distinguish a journal from a diary, saying:

> A diary is a record of daily events in one's own life. The journal may take as its starting point the same events as a diary, but in journaling, one looks inward to see how one is affected by the events. (Broyles 1988, 12)

Written to be used by individuals or small groups, it presents six different approaches to the discipline. These include reflection on supposedly mundane events, interaction with biblical passages, recording of guided meditations, dream recording, interaction with general reading, and musing over daily conversations. A chapter of guided exercises is devoted to each of these options, with blank pages included for practice. The book is full of scriptural references and exercises. Of some concern is the author's failure to provide safety guidelines for the use of the imagination.

Adventure Inward: Christian Growth through Personal Journal Writing was written by Morton T. Kelsey (1980). Refusing to accept the stereotype that journaling is drudgery, he says: "A journal properly used is like a playground into which we can step and play when we are alone" (Kelsey 1980, 20). Kelsey emphasizes the need to record interactions with God so that their outworkings in later events cannot be easily dismissed. An especially good chapter faces some potential dangers of journaling. Among these is automatic writing, inflated ego over presumed divine connections, demonic influence, and repetitious reflection without action. A weakness in the book is the authority that the author assigns to dreams.

Joyce Chapman has contributed *Journaling for Joy: Writing Your Way to Personal Growth and Freedom* (1991). The greatest strength of this work is its many examples of journal entries. It also focuses extensively on inner reflection. Not written from a Christian standpoint, it encourages an extreme self-centeredness. Another weakness is its obsession with the pursuit of joy, which believers should realize is not an end in itself.

George F. Simons is the author of *Journal for Life: Discovering Faith and Values Through Journal Keeping* (1975). Its first volume contains basic strategies for spiritual growth while its second volume encourages the development of experiential theology. The progression within the volumes is logical and well-guided by dozens of questions. It encourages reflection on both positive and negative characteristics of one's self. A weakness of Simon's work is his view that modern academic disciplines make it impossible to take the Bible literally, a view that makes his guidance very subjective.

The Journal of John Woolman and a Plea for the Poor (Woolman 1972) records the experiences of an eighteenth century Quaker business man and preacher. The journal records Woolman's reflections concerning, and actions on behalf of, slaves, indentured servants, and exploited children. It also contains a few accounts of intimate interactions with God. This book still is more representative of a ministry diary than of a journal of spiritual interaction between a man and his God.

The Journal of John Wesley (Wesley n.d.) was written by the eighteenth century founder of Methodism. It spans a period of fifty-five years of ministry. It reveals Wesley as a man of enormous energy and uncompromising standards. Persecution, travel, and ministry successes are recorded. The journal contains little on the personal devotional life of its author.

The Asian Journal of Thomas Merton (Merton 1968) contains reflections of a Catholic monk while on a 1968 trip to Thailand. It records a mixture of simple events, meditations, poems, and letters. Merton uses little, if any, Scripture and exhibits an alarming openness to Zen Buddhism.

Fasting

God's Chosen Fast: A Spiritual and Practical Guide to Fasting (Wallis 1968) is an excellent treatise on the subject from both the scriptural and practical viewpoints. The largest portion of the book is given to an extensive biblical presentation of the discipline. The normal, absolute, and partial fasts are dealt with, along with fasting for holiness, prayer answers, evangelism, deliverance, and revelation. Practical chapters deal with how to begin and end fasts, and how to keep a diary of a fast. The appendix includes a section on doubtful references to fasting, as well as helpful pages answering questions about, and objections to, the practice. Physical benefits of this discipline are discussed, with scientific verification from medical sources. Wallis is transparent in his desire not to overstate his case and, thus, his work represents a well-balanced approach to a much-neglected discipline.

Fasting Changed My Life (Anderson 1977) is more than a testimonial. The author begins his book with records of fasting in the lives of historic church figures such as Murray, Brainerd, Torrey, Wesley, and Finney. After laying a firm foundation from the Bible, Anderson mentions several results of fasting. Among these are victory over temptation, a more profound realization of God's presence, more effective prayer, vision for ministry, and revelation of God's will. A section dealing with cautions in fasting is most helpful. Here the reader is told to be careful of health, poor attitudes, ritual practice of the discipline, and self-deception. The author's own experience and vulnerability add to the credibility of his work. A section of testimonials to the power of fasting includes comments by modern Christian leaders such as Charles Stanley and Jack R. Taylor.

Fasting: What the Bible Teaches (Falwell 1981) is full of scriptural support. Its four chapters deal with why the believer should fast, biblical foundations, how to fast, and breaking the fast. In addressing proper motivation for the fast, he says:

> The credibility of fasting is not in the abstention from food but in the sincerity of the person who manifests his faith by withholding himself from food. . . . When a person believes that God will be honored by the dedication of his body, the time spent in prayer, and the abstinence from food, his fasting becomes an act of faith. (Falwell 1981, 30)

Fasting in the Orthodox Church: Its Theological, Pastoral, and Social Implications (Akakios 1990) considers abstention from food as practiced in the Eastern Orthodox Church. The author's knowledge of the patristic witness is extensive, reaching back to Tertullian at A. D. 220. Scriptural references abound. An especially good chapter is entitled, "Fasting and Pastoral Concerns." It demonstrates correlation between fasting and high church attendance. It also suggests, without claiming too much, that fasting promotes mental health and concern for the needy. A reader who will look beyond the sectarianism, and occasional legalism, in this work may acquire both historical perspective and practical appreciation for the discipline.

Fasting, Longevity, and Immortality (Johnson 1978) approaches the exercise from the standpoint of personal experience, clinical studies, and speculative projections. Johnson's extensive accounts of his own prolonged fasts, and his explanation of physical phenomena during them, make interesting reading. However, his radically extended fasts, disposition for psychic experiences, and pantheism, make this book a potential danger zone for its readers.

"Fasting and Bodily Preparation—A Fine Outward Training" (Fischer 1959) was published in the *Concordia Theological Journal*. It surveys the practice from the time of Moses to the present. Fischer demonstrates from Scripture that believers have fasted during times of distress, anger, disappointment, repentance, and mourning. He also traces the development of fasting traditions, such as lent. The teaching of Martin Luther on the subject is dealt with in detail, especially his stress on avoiding legalism and pretense.

"The Practice of Fasting in the New Testament," (Mitchell 1990) ran in *Bibliotheca Sacra*. It is important for its hermeneutical approach to the issue. Seeking to ascertain if and when the practice is legitimate for today, Mitchell surveys the pertinent scriptural passages. He concludes that fasting is never required of New Testament believers, although it may be used as an expression of humility and repentance in times of danger, trials, heartaches, or sorrows. Some readers will not feel comfortable with his attempt to dismiss fasting as an aid to prayer and guidance while making critical decisions.

Bible Study

Since the Bible is the believer's authoritative guide on the spiritual journey, it is the ground out of which spiritual disciplines should develop. A few basic guides to biblical study are mentioned in this section.

Methodical Bible Study: A New Approach to Hermeneutics (Traina 1952) deals extensively with four steps in the study process: observation, interpretation, application, and correlation. Sixteen "literary relations" are given to guide the process of observation. Appendices include tips on charting, word studies, and outlines. This is arguably the best work available on the subject.

The Joy of Discovery in Bible Study (Wald 1975) is concisely organized under the verbs observe, interpret, summarize, evaluate, apply, and actualize. Readers are guided through several passages using the methods described. A small, but excellent, chapter is given to application (principle level) and actualization.

Howard F. Vos wrote *Effective Bible Study: A Guide to Sixteen Methods* (1956). It is a survey of major approaches to Bible study including the analytic, synthetic, inductive, critical, historical, scientific, and psychological approaches, among others. Perhaps these "methods" should all be presented as aspects of one thorough study of a passage, rather than as separate disciplines. A helpful section on filing study notes may be found in the appendix.

How to Understand Your Bible (Sterrett 1974) is given to helping people interpret the English Bible. It discusses spiritual qualifications, Bible versions, and study aids needed for effective study. Good sections on figures of speech and symbols are included. A weakness is the failure to lay a foundation for interpretation in observational techniques or even to allude to them.

Protestant Biblical Interpretations: A Textbook of Hermeneutics (Ramm 1970) is a scholarly treatise on the history and process of interpretation. Under qualifications for an interpreter, Ramm includes being born again, having a passion for God's Word, and having a deep reverence for God. An excellent chapter of guidelines is given for the devotional use of Scripture. Some will be disappointed with the author's failure to consistently employ a literal method in the interpretation of prophetic Scripture.

Validity in Interpretation (Hirsch 1967), not a Christian work per se, is given to valid approaches to the interpretation of literature in general. A major contribution is its discussion of issues surrounding authorial intent. Hirsch argues that the text means what the author means, that the author's meaning is accessible, and that the author knows what he means.

The Literature of the Bible (Ryken 1974) was written to help Bible readers feel more comfortable with its many genres. Scripture is extensively analyzed under seventeen categories of subject matter. While he sees different genres present, Ryken still argues that the Holy Scripture should be viewed as a unified whole.

Read Through the Bible in a Year (Kohlenberger 1986) is an excellent guide to systematic reading. The reading schedule integrates biblical passages chronologically, giving many readers a perspective on Scripture that they have never possessed previously. It also provides a simple summary of each book.

The New Unger's Bible Handbook (Unger 1984) is Gary N. Larson's revision of the classic work of Merrill F. Unger. Detailed introductions are provided for each book of the Bible. Pertinent archaeological information, supporting the biblical text, abounds. Historical background for the books is developed and a section on the intertestmental period is included. An excellent description of how the Bible came to us is also present.

The Moody Atlas of Bible Lands (Beitzel 1985) includes ninety-five vivid, colorful maps, which present the geography of the lands of the Bible. It is marked by conservative scholarship and extensive description.

The effect of Bible reading on social behavior is the topic of the *Christianity Today* article "What's the Connection Between Faith and Works?" (Brown 1980). The author cites evidence, from a Gallup poll, in concluding that regular Bible readers are significantly more involved in general volunteerism, visitation of sick and elderly persons, charitable giving, and political-ethical issues than the general public.

Simplicity

Freedom of Simplicity (Foster 1981) was written to cultivate inward and outward singleness of heart in its readers. Foster shows, from Scripture, that simplicity is both timeless and relevant as a spiritual discipline. Beginning with the need for inward simplicity, shown in quietness and contentment before God, the author advances to the outward manifestation of simple and sacrificial living, voluntary poverty, planned spending, separation from consumptiveness, and ethical investing are placed before the reader for consideration. Challenges are also issued to churches and business corporations. All of this is done, however, without a legalistic tone.

The Challenge of the Disciplined Life: Christian Reflections on Money, Sex, and Power (1985) was also authored by Foster. The section on money deals with both its dangers and benefits. It warns against using money to create a base of power, while urging sacrificial giving and recognition of God as owner of all wealth. An excellent section discusses the ethical use of money in business. The author is not as specific as he might have been, in his discussion of Luke 16, where disciples are commanded to use money particularly for evangelism.

Ronald J. Sider edited *Living More Simply: Biblical Principles and Practical Models* (1980). It represents a compilation of papers presented at the U.S. Consultation on Simple Lifestyle in April 1979. The material is challenging from both the philosophical and practical aspects. Practical suggestions include buying inexpensive appliances and cars, going without televisions, turning the furnace down considerably, and sharing a lawn mower. The authors caution that commitment to such a lifestyle should not be faddish, legalistic, or prideful. While much is to be gained from these articles, many readers will disagree with the notion that "evangelism and social action are equal and full partners in the mission of God's people" (1980, 165).

"A Rich, Full Life: Discipline, Simple Living, and the Gospel" (Alexander 1987) was published in *The Other Side* It is a light-hearted attempt to apply the "middle class value" of discipline to a poverty-level lifestyle. Dismissing good intentions as an adequate excuse for failure, he challenges the reader to action. Soda and candy bars, coffee and donuts, stereos, computers, books—may have to go, he says, if hungry children are to be fed.

"Challenging Christians to the Simple Life" (Gaebelein 1979) was written for *Christianity Today*. Gaebelein criticizes Evangelicals for claiming ownership of what is really God's, and for undue selectivity in preaching, which avoids confrontation concerning social issues. Based on the Old Testament, he builds a case for living less materialistically. A major premise is the need to find human dignity in our creation in God's image, not in wealth or position.

"Journey toward Simple Living" (Granberg-Michaelson 1980) appeared in *The Other Side*. It chronicles a middle-class couple's struggle to lower its monetary lifestyle. Michaelson found that her shopping and eating habits were undisciplined when she felt spiritually unfulfilled. Her solutions included fellowship with a community of believes committed to simplicity, using the More With Less Cookbook, and, most of all, acknowledging that only God could meet her deepest needs.

"Lessons on the Simple Life" (Olsen 1984) ran in *One World* and concerns the missionary experiences of the author's sister and brother-in-law in Upper Volta. In that location they learned the beauty of worship in a plain chapel, the appreciation of simple clothing, and the lessons inherent in sharing a home with others. Their service taught them a higher respect for people and a lower respect for things.

"Learning to Live with Money" (Yancey 1984) was written for *Christianity Today*. The article records the writer's struggle to find middle ground between simplicity and excess. He expresses his discomfort with what he sees as political bias and distortion of Scripture among many who urge simple lifestyles. He defends capitalism as a system and notes that American consumption fuels the economies of many otherwise destitute nations. He also shares transparently concerning a period of time in his life when he became too enamored with money and its management. Yancey found balance in joyful, sacrificial, giving and in depending on God's gracious guidance in living.

Practicing the Presence

The leading work on this discipline continues to be *The Practice of the Presence of God* (Lawrence 1979). Written by a seventeenth century monk, it epitomizes what it means to live and to serve daily in God's presence. The book consists of letters from and about Brother Lawrence, telling of his encounters with God in nature and in his ministry as a kitchen servant.

Contemplative Prayer (Merton 1969) was written by a Catholic monk. While primarily for those devoted to monastic life, it is of benefit to all contemplatives. Of contemplation he says:

> Hence monastic prayer, especially meditation and contemplative prayer, is not so much a way to find God, as a way of resting in him whom we have found, who loves us, who is near to us, who comes to draw us to himself. (Merton 1969, 29)

Increased awareness of God's presence, Merton states, is the main purpose for solitude and silence. The desire for the experience of God, however, does not justify acting on how we feel, says the author. Experience must be consistent with Scripture. Readers should beware of the author's penchant for eastern religions.

Merton also wrote *Seeds of Contemplation* (1949), an extensive reflection on God, who can be seen at work in all aspects of a believer's life. The value of this work is that it shows how deep and mature the thoughts of an experienced contemplative can become. It is Merton's basic contribution to the field.

Practicing the Presence (Goldsmith 1958) was written because, in contemplation, the author found relief from feelings of failure, unhappiness, and dissatisfaction with life. Even the introduction of the book is exciting as it leaves no doubt as to the change that unceasing prayer can bring to a life. While the author uses Scripture extensively, it is disappointing to find him lapse, on occasion, into universalism.

Tilden Edwards is the writer of *Living in the Presence: Disciplines for the Spiritual Heart* (1987). Edwards sees a divided heart as the greatest hindrance to experiencing God's presence. Recognition of pride and reliance on the Holy Spirit help to create a whole heart, he says. Numerous practical exercises are found in the book. Its unusually good contributions are instructions on practicing the presence in a group and on preparing individuals to lead such groups. One potential danger is the author's encouragement to use icons in the development of the spiritual imagination.

The Cloud of Unknowing is of uncertain authorship, although evidence exists that this writer was a fourteenth century priest (Magill and McGreal 1988, 186). Personal helplessness, intense focus on loving God, and pure conscience are seen as essential to a deepening sense of God's presence. Written as from a mentor, the reader can easily receive the book as personal instruction. A weakness is the disorderly presentation of material.

"Searching for Real Presence" (Malone 1991) appeared in *Leadership*. It is concerned with how a sense of God's presence may be gained in congregational worship. Openly inviting the Holy Spirit's presence, using songs that address God in the second person, and more frequent use of the Lord's Supper are among the author's suggestions.

"Practicing the Presence in the Pastorate" (Bridston 1988) was penned for *Leadership*. It deals with the problem of integrating prayer life with a busy pastoral schedule. His solution is unexpected: recognize God as being gracious and delight in relationship with him. The whole day then becomes a series of conversations with a loved one. Bridston concludes by saying: "I discovered God is my Friend, not my Foreman" (Bridston 1988, 31).

Confession

Confess Your Sins: The Way of Reconciliation (Stott 1964) lays a solid biblical foundation for the practice of confession. It considers secret confession (to God), private confession (to an offended individual), and public confession (to the church). Each section includes scriptural support and practical advice. Spiritual and psychological benefits of the practice are highlighted. An excellent discussion of the concept of auricular confession (to a priest) is included, the author deciding against the practice.

Confession of Sin (MacArthur 1986) is an exposition of 1 John 1:1—2:2. It deals thoroughly with the nature, affects, and forgiveness of sins. Helpful review and application sections conclude the various pericopes. Some will find the author's interpretation of 1:9, as positional truth, to be controversial.

The Dynamics of Confession (Bowman 1969) draws on the author's experience as a pastor and hospital chaplain. He deals with confession as it relates to the alleviation of guilt, and subsequent mental health. He discusses true and false guilt, the affect of personality on confessional approach, and the confessant's view of God, as these issues influence the process. Bowman tells how a nondirective approach can help draw out confession and bring spiritual relief. This is a valuable contribution in the effort to bring theological soundness to the practice of psychological care.

The Confessions of Saint Augustine (Augustine 1949) is an example of candid confession. The work consists of thirteen "books," nine of which recount sins such as thievery, sexual immorality, and selfishness. While most of the sins occurred before Augustine's conversion, the book still helpfully reflects human depravity and sin's destructive power. It also highlights God's grace and can encourage readers to keep a clean conscience before him.

The Confessions of Jacob Boehme (Boehme 1954) contains the frankly admitted spiritual struggles of a seventeenth century mystic. Such impediments to spiritual growth as the flesh, satanic opposition, and failing emotions are noted. Boehme admits to anger, covetousness, and malice; but he also records times of great spiritual victory. This balance helps the believer to see his own struggle in a realistic way. A weakness of the book is Boehme's penchant for an extreme mysticism that often leads him into subjectivity.

Confession: The Road to Forgiveness (Murray 1983) is a treatment of Psalm 51. It is concerned with the themes of brokenness, complete forgiveness, and subsequent joy. It is valuable devotionally while maintaining theological accuracy.

"A Celebration Feast of Forgiveness" (Burquest 1982) appeared in *Christianity Today*. This article deals with the felt need of many Christians, especially Protestants, to confess sin to others and to be assured of God's forgiveness by others. This, he says, can be done without forsaking the priesthood of the individual. His solution is to affirm God's forgiveness communally in the celebration of the Lord's Supper. Thus communion becomes not only remembrance, but public celebration of accepted confession.

"The Value of Confession and Forgiveness According to Jung" (Todd 1985) ran in the *Journal of Religion and Health* and focuses on the psychological benefits of confession. The author discusses the Jungian conviction that public confession is more effective than secret confession in restoring mental health. While no claim can be made for Jung's Christianity, two biblical truths surface in his study. First, a dichotomy of psychology and spirituality is invalid. Second, the practice of confessing faults to one another is valid.

Petition

Works listed here focus on requests for self and others, as well as some general works on prayer.

The Struggle of Prayer (Bloesch 1988b) is special for the great number of issues it covers intelligently yet succinctly. Bloesch examines the scriptural basis for prayer, considering the roles of Jesus Christ and the Holy Spirit in the process. He wrestles with issues such as unanswered prayer, striving with God, magical thinking, and prayer and action. He also deals extensively with the significant differences in the approaches of mysticism and pietism to the subject.

Teach Us to Pray: Prayer in the Bible and the World (Carson 1990) contains the contributions of twenty evangelical scholars, from around the world, focused on four broad subject areas: biblical theology of prayer, prayer and spirituality, lessons in prayer from the world-wide church, and the challenge to pray. This book represents an excellent treatment of both foundational and experiential aspects of the subject.

A Diary of Private Prayer (Baillie 1949) is offered as a guide to private prayer in devotional life. It is full of petition for intimacy with God and for personal sanctification. It also includes honest confessions and generous praise. It is conveniently arranged with morning and evening prayers for each day of the month. Blank pages are provided for the reader's own specific requests.

Bill Hybel's *Too Busy Not to Pray: Slowing Down to Be With God* (Hybels 1988) is a practical guide to developing a prayer life amid a hectic schedule. While candid about his own failings, Hybels gives pointers on establishing a prayer time, practicing the presence, and discerning the source of inner promptings. He also presents the various types of prayer in clear terms for the average layperson.

"The Effects of Prayer and Prayer Experiences on Measures of General Well-Being" (Poloma and Pendleton 1981) is a research article that appeared in the *Journal of Psychology and Theology*. Its importance lies in the fact that it establishes an objective link between various forms of prayer and positive adjustment to difficult life situations. Prayer is not a "neurotic flight from the unpleasant" (Poloma and Pendleton 1981, 72). It also shows that certain forms of prayer affect certain aspects of adjustment. Meditative prayer positively impacted existential well-being and religious satisfaction, colloquial prayer (for guidance, blessing, confession, expression of love) affected happiness. Ritual prayer had a definite negative influence. The article also establishes that how one prays, and what one prays, is more important than how often one prays.

"Pastoral Counseling and Petitionary Prayer" (Morgan 1987) was written for the *Journal of Religion and Health*. He addresses the effect of intercession on the spiritual healing of parishioners. Prayer is seen as the logical response to compassion for counselees. The recognition of God's presence throughout the whole process of guidance is understood as the key to releasing the pastor from the burden of the healer's role.

"Petitionary Prayer and the Character of God" (Cousar 1986) ran in *Journal for Preachers*. Its thesis is that petitionary prayer is essentially calling God to account for divine promises made. Referring to such passages as Luke 18:1–8, Matt 6:9–10, and Exod 32:7–14, the author presents a case for urging God, based on his character, to keep his Word. Contending with God, in prayer, is sanctioned. This article does not run from the problems of prayer. It finds their solution in the person of God.

Celebration

The titles listed here encompass enjoyment of life in God, praise, and thanksgiving.

Praise (Allen 1983) encourages a life of praise grounded not in ideal circumstances but in obedience to God. The teaching is set in the framework of the author's own processing of trials, including the leukemia of his baby daughter. The thematic verse for the booklet is Ps 146:3: "While I live I will praise the Lord, I will sing praises to God while I have my being."

Celebrate the Temporary (Reid 1974) calls the reader to rejoice in the common gifts of God in creation such as children, flowers, food, trees, rain, and friends. Illustrated poetry appears throughout the book. The author's involvement in the human potential movement presents a potential danger for the novice.

"More is Less: Add Some Celebration to Your Life" (Sine 1988) appeared in *The Other Side*. It is an invitation to Christian joy. In the author's words, "We're headed for a party to end all parties, so let's start living like it now" (1988, 37). He illustrates ways of celebrating our Christian heritage such as biblical masquerade parties, drama, and banqueting. He suggests such joy will draw outsiders to Christ.

The *Christian Scholars Review* published "Towards a Christian Play Ethic" (Holmes 1981). The author sees play as more an attitude, or state of mind, than a distinguishable set of activities. He also develops a theology of play based on God's enjoyment of creation, the provision of a Sabbath for his people, and the joys of the coming kingdom. Paraphrasing Aquinas, he says: "play should have positive moral and other consequences, it should be properly controlled, and it should be both timely and worthily human" (Holmes 1981, 47).

"The Pointlessness of Praise" (Willimon 1989) is a sermon that was published by *Christian Ministry*. Its preacher shows clearly that praise is often not simply a matter of the will, as in obedience to exhortation. Rather, it is reflexive and responsive. It should burst forth out of a focus on God. When we get our minds off ourselves, he says, praise will result.

The *Journal of Theology for Southern Africa* ran "On Thanking God Whatever Happens" (Brummer 1984). It argues that gratitude should be the result of reflecting on God's attributes. Since God is omnipotent and his intentions are good, we should thank him in all the events of our lives. Praise will become a habit as we interpret all events in light of faith, acknowledging God's fellowship with us whatever happens.

Bibliography

Akakios, Archimandrite. 1990. *Fasting in the Orthodox Church*. Etna: Center For Traditionalist Orthodox Studies.

Alexander, John. 1987. A rich, full life: Discipline, simple living, and the gospel. *The Other Side* 23 (January–February): 14–15.

Allen, Ronald B. 1983. *Praise*. Portland: Multnomah.

Anderson, Andy. 1977. *Fasting changed my life*. Nashville: Broadman.

Anderson, Neil T. 1991. *Walking through the darkness*. San Bernadino: Here's Life.

Anderson, Neil T., and Steve Russo. 1991. *The seduction of our children*. Eugene: Harvest House.

Anderson, Paul. 1988. Selling ancient disciplines to moderns. *Leadership* 9 (Fall): 18–19.

Arens, Edmund. 1985. Jesus' communicative actions: The basis for Christian faith praxis, witnessing, and confessing. *Conrad Grebel Review* 3 (Winter): 67–85.

Arnold, Eberhard. 1985. Why we choose silence over dialogue. *The Plough* 11 (July–August): 12.

Augustine. 1949. *The confessions of Saint Augustine*. New York: Random House.

Baillie, John. 1949. *A diary of private prayer*. Mew York: Macmillan.

Barrois, George A. 1947. Mysticism—what is it? *Theology Today* 4: 190–202.

Basset, Rodney L., Ronald D. Sadler, Eric E. Kobischen, David M. Skiff, Ivy J. Merrill, Barbara J. Atwater, and Paul W. Livermore. 1981. The shepherd scale: Separating the sheep from the goats. *Journal of Psychology and Theology* 9 (Winter): 335–351.

Beitzel, Barry. 1985. *The Moody atlas of Bible lands*. Chicago: Moody.

Belton, Francis George. 1936. *A manual for confessors*. London and Oxford: Mowbray.

Benner, David G. 1988. *Psychotherapy and the spiritual quest*. Grand Rapids: Baker.

Benson, Bob, and Michael W. Benson. 1989. *Disciplines for the inner life*. Nashville: Generoux-Nelson.

Bittinger, Emmert F. 1978. The simple life: A chapter in the evolution of a doctrine. *Brethren Life and Thought* 23 (Spring): 104–114.

Bloesch, Donald G. 1988a. *The crisis of piety: Essays toward a theology of the Christian life*. Colorado Springs: Helmers and Howard. 1988b. *The struggle of prayer*. Colorado Springs: Helmers and Howard 1991. Lost in the mystical myths. *ChristianityToday*, 19 August, 22–24.

Boehme, Jacob. 1954. *The confessions of Jacob Boehme*. New York: Gordon.

Booker, Richard. 1983. *Intimacy with God*. South Plainfield: Bridge.

Bowman, George William. 1969. *The dynamics of confession*. Richmond: John Knox.

Bridston, Richard. 1988. Practicing the presence in the pastorate. *Leadership* 9 (Fall): 31.

Brock, Fred R. Jr. 1975. *The power of prayer*. Des Plaines: Regular Baptist Press.

Brown, Harold O. J. 1980. What's the connection between faith and works? *Christianity Today*, 24 October, 26–29.

Broyles, Anne. 1988. *Journaling: A spirit journey*. Nashville: The Upper Room.

Brummer, Vincent. 1984. On thanking God whatever happens. *Journal of Theology for Southern Africa* 48 (September): 3–12.

Burquest, Donald A. 1982. A celebration feast of forgiveness. *Christianity Today*, 9 April, 24–25.

Calvin, John. 1948. *Commentaries on the epistles of Paul the apostle to the Philippians, Colossians, and Thessalonians*. Grand Rapids: Eerdmans.

Carson, D. A., ed. 1990. *Teach us to pray: Prayer in the Bible and in the world*. Grand Rapids: Baker.

Chafer, Lewis Sperry. 1967. *He that is spiritual*. Grand Rapids: Zondervan.

Chambers, Oswald. 1947. *The psychology of redemption*. London: Simpkin Marshall.

Chapman, Joyce. 1991. *Journaling for joy*. North Hollywood: Newcastle Publishing Company.

Clinebell, Howard. 1965. *Mental health through Christian community*. Nashville: Abingdon.

Cooper, Emmett. 1991. Sweeter than honey. *Kindred Spirit*, Autumn, 14–15.

Corduan, Winfried. 1991. *Mysticism: An evangelical option?*
Grand Rapids: Zondervan.

Cornwall, Faith. 1981. Healing through solitude and community. *Quarterly Review* 1 (Summer): 77–85.

Cousar, Charles B. 1986. Petitionary prayer and the character of God. *Journal for Preachers* 9 (Pentecost): 11–15.

Cowan, Arthur A. 1952. Unqualified praise. *The Expository Times* 62 (August): 344–346.

Crocker, Sylvia Fleming. 1984. Prayer as *a* model of communication. *Pastoral Psychology* 33 (Winter): 83–93.

Day, Albert E. 1961. *Discipline and discovery*. Nashville: Parthenon.

DeHaan, Kurt, and Dan Vander Lugt. 1990. *What's the appeal of the New Age movement?* Grand Rapids: Radio Bible class.

Demarest, Bruce. 1991. Devotion, doctrine, and duty in Dietrich Bonhoeffer. *Bibliotheca Sacra* 148 (October–December): 399–408.

Demarest, Bruce, and Charles Raup. 1989. Recovering the heart of Christian spirituality. *Criswell Theological Review* 3:321–325.

deMello, Anthony. 1984. *Sadhana: A way to God*. New York: Image Press.

Denison, Charles S.1992. Soulwork: How to strengthen the ministry from the inside out. *Leadership* 13 (Spring) 104–108.

Denny, Randal E. 1987. *Intimacy with God*. Kansas City, MO: Beacon Hill.

Dent, Barbara. 1990. Of oak tree roots and submarines: Reflections on the dark night. *Spiritual Life* 236 (Spring): 11–145.

Dieter, Melvin E., Anthony A. Hoekema, Stanley M. Horton, J. Robertson McQuilken, and John F. Walvoord. 1987. *Five views on sanctification*. Grand Rapids: Zondervan.

Downing, Jim. 1976. *Meditation*. Colorado Springs: Navpress.

Eckhart, Meister. 1941. *Meister Eckhart*. Translated by Raymond Blakney. New York: Harper.

Edwards, Tilden H. 1987. *Living in the presence: Disciplines for the spiritual heart*. San Francisco: HarperCollins.

Egan, Harvey D. 1984. *Christian mysticism: The future of a tradition*. New York: Pueblo.

Ellison, Craig W. 1983. Spiritual well–being: Conceptualization and measurement. *Journal of Psychology and Theology* 11 (Winter): 330–340.

Falwell, Jerry. 1981.*Fasting: What the Bible teaches*. Wheaton: Tyndale.

Faw, Bill. 1984. Simple life concepts in Brethren history. Brethren *Life and Thought* 2 9 (Summer): 152–157.

Felker, Steven D. 1988. Type b spirituality. *Leadership 9* (Fall): 21.

Fischer, Walter F. 1959. Fasting and bodily preparation—a fine outward training. *Concordia Theological Journal* 30 (December): 887–901.

Forsyth, P. T. 1957. *God the Holy Father*. London: Independent.

Foster, Richard J. 1981. *Freedom of simplicity*. San Francisco: HarperCollins 1983.

———. *Meditative prayer*. Downers Grove: InterVarsity 1985.

———. *The challenge of the disciplined life: Christian reflections on money, sex, and power*. San Francisco: HarperCollins 1988. *Celebration of discipline: The path to spiritual growth*. Rev. ed. San Francisco: Harper & Row 1990.

———. Spiritual challenges. *Christian Herald* 113 (January–February): 16–17.

Freeman, Harold. 1987. *Variety in biblical preaching*. Waco: Word.

Gaebelein, Frank E. 1979. Challenging Christians to the simple life. *Christianity Today*, 21 September, 22–29.

Goforth, Rosalind. 1921. *How I know God answers prayer*. Grand Rapids: Zondervan.

Goldsmith, Joel S. 1958. *Practicing the presence*. New York: Harper & Row 1963. *The contemplative life*. New York: Julian Press.

Granberg-Michaelson, Karin. 1980. Journey toward simple living. *The Other Side* 16 (November): 39–41.

Green, Thomas H. 1981. *Darkness in the marketplace*. Notre Dame: Ava Maria Press.

Groeschel, Benedict J. 1989. *Spiritual passages: The psychology of spiritual development*. New York: Crossroad.

Groothuis, Douglas R. 1986. *Unmasking the new age*. Downers Grove: InterVarsity.

Guiness, Os. 1983. *The gravedigger file*. Downers Grove: InterVarsity.

Guyon, Madame. 1975. *Experiencing the depths of Jesus Christ*. Beaumont: Seed Sowers.

Happold, F. C. 1963. *Mysticism: A study and an anthology*. Middlesex: Penguin Books.

Hardman, O. 1924. *The ideals of asceticism: An essay in the comparative study of religion*. New York: Macmillan.

Harkness, Georgia. 1973. *Mysticism: Its meaning and its message*. Nashville: Abingdon.

Hauser, Richard J. 1986. *Moving in the Spirit: Becoming a contemplative in action*. New York: Paulist.

Hayford, Jack, John Huffman, J.I. Packer, and Chuck Swindoll. 1991. The power and the presence. *Leadership* 12 (Summer); 14–23.

Hestenes, Roberta. 1988. Can spiritual maturity be taught? *Leadership* 9 (Pall): 12–20.

Hingley, C. J. H. 1990. Evangelicals and spirituality. *Themelios* (April–May): 86–91.

Hinson, E. Glenn. 1979. *The Reaffirmation of prayer*. Nashville: Broadman.

Hirsch, E. D. 1967. *Validity in interpretation*. New Haven: Yale University Press.

Hogue, Harland E. 1969. *Prayer: The vital center*. Berkley, CA: United Church Press.

Holmes, Arthur F. 1981. Towards a Christian play ethic. *Christian Scholar's Review* 11:41–50.

Holmes, Urban T. 1980. *A history of Christian spirituality*. New York: Seabury 1982. *Spirituality for ministry*. San Francisco: Harper & Row.

Houston, J. M., ed. 1984. Spirituality. In *Evangelical dictionary of theology*. Walter A. Elwell, 1050. Grand Rapids: Baker.

Hubbard-McNall, Julie. 1991. Breaking free: The experience of solitude. *American Baptist Quarterly* 10 (June): 148–150.

Hughes, Philip Edgcumbe. 1977. *Commentary on the epistle to the Hebrews*. Grand Rapids: Eerdmans.

Hughes, R. Kent. 1991. *Disciplines of a godly man*. Wheaton: Crossway.

Hybels, Bill. 1988. *Too busy not to pray: Slowing down to be with God*. Downers Grove: InterVarsity.

Inge, W. R. 1924. *Personal religion and the life of devotion*. London: Longmans and Green.

Johnson, Arthur L. 1988. *Faith misguided: Exposing the dangers of mysticism*. Chicago: Moody.

Johnson, Charles W. 1978. *Fasting, longevity, and immortality.* Turkey Hills: Survival Publishing Company.

Johnston, William. 1990. *Lord, teach us to pray: Christian Zen and the inner eye of love.* London: Fount Paperbacks.

Jones, Cheslyn, Geoffrey Wainwright, and Edward Yarnold, eds. 1986. *The study of spirituality.* New York: Oxford University Press.

Jones, E. Stanley. 1968. *Song of ascents.* Nashville: Abingdon.

Jung, Carl. 1933. *Modern man in search of a soul.* New York: Harcourt and Brace.

Kelly, Thomas R. 1941. *A testament of devotion.* New York: Harper & Row.

Kelsey, Morton T. 1976. *The other side of silence.* New York: Paulist 1980. *Adventure inward.* Minneapolis: Augsburg 1982. *Christo-psychology.* New York: Crossroad.

Kempis, Thomas A. 1984. *The imitation of Christ.* Westwood: The Christian Library.

Killinger, John. 1976. *Bread for the wilderness.* Waco: Word.

Klug, Ronald. 1982. *How to keep a spiritual journal.* Nashville: Thomas Nelson.

Kohlenberger, John R. 1986. *Read through the Bible in a year.* Chicago: Moody.

Kroll, Woodrow. 1991. Getting to know God. *Prokope* 8 (January—February): 1–2.

LaHaye, Tim. 1976. *How to study the Bible for yourself.* Irvine: Harvest House.

Laidlaw, J. 1895. *The Bible and the doctrine of man.* Edinburgh: T & T Clark.

Law, William. 1966. *A serious call to a devout and holy life.* Grand Rapids: Eerdmans.

Lawrence, Brother. 1977. *The practice of the presence of God.* New York: Doubleday.

Leech, Kenneth. 1977. *Soul friend.* San Francisco: Harper & Row 1985. *Experiencing God: Theology as spirituality.* San Francisco: Harper & Row.

Lewis, C. S. 1961. *The screwtape letters.* New York: Macmillan.

Lewis, Gordon. 1989. *Distinguishing Christianity from New Age spiritual experience.* CP2028. Trinity Evangelical Divinity School.

Lloyd-Jones, D. Martyn. 1965. *Spiritual depression.* Grand Rapids: Eerdmans.

Lovelace, Richard F. 1979. *Dynamics of spiritual life.* Downers Grove:InterVarsity 1988. Evangelical spirituality: A church historian's perspective. *Journal of the Evangelical Theological Society* 31 (March): 25–35.

Lundquist, Carl H. 1990. *Christian spirituality: A selected bibliography.* St. Paul: Evangelical Order of the Burning Heart.

MacArthur, John. 1986. *Confession of sin.* Chicago: Moody.

MacDonald, Gordon. 1984. *Ordering your private world.* Nashville: Nelson.

Magill, Frank N., and Ian P. McGreal, eds. 1988. *Christian spirituality: The essential guide to the most influential spiritual writings of the Christian tradition.* San Francisco: Harper & Row.

Magnuson, Sally. 1981. *The flying Scotsman.* New York: QuartetPublishing Company.

Malone, George. 1991. Searching for real presence. *Leadership* 12 (Summer): 42–44.

Mayhall, Carole. 1976. From *the heart of a woman.* Colorado Springs: Navpress.

McBride, Neal F. 1990. *How to lead small groups.* Colorado Springs: Navpress.

Mead, Frank S., ed. 1965. *Encyclopedia of religious quotations.* London: Peter Davis.

Meadow, Mary Jo. 1984. The dark side of mysticism: Depression and "the dark night". *Pastoral Psychology* 33 (Winter): 105–123.

Merton, Thomas. 1948. *The seven storey mountain.* New York: Harcourt and Brace 1949. *Seeds of contemplation.* New York: New Directions 1961. *The new man.* New York: Farrar, Straus, and Gudahy 1968. *The Asian journal of Thomas Merton.* New York: New Directions 1969. *Contemplative prayer.* Garden City: Doubleday.

Meyer, F. B. 1985. *Changed by the master's touch.* Springdale Whitaker. *Secrets of Christian living.* Westchester: Good News.

Miller, Calvin. 1977. *Transcendental hesitation: A biblical appraisal of TM and eastern mysticism*. Grand Rapids: Zondervan. 1984. *The table of inwardness*. Downers Grove: InterVarsity.

Minirth, Frank. 1977. *Christian psychiatry*. Old Tappan: Revell.

Minirth, Frank, Donald Hawkins, Paul Meijer, and Richard Flournoy. 1986. *How to beat burnout*. Chicago: Moody.

Mitchell, Curtis. 1990. The practice of fasting in the New Testament. *Bibliotheca Sacra* 147 (October–December): 455–469.

Montgomery, John M. 1987. *Money, power, greed: Has the church been sold out?* Ventura: Regal Books.

Moon, Gary W., and John Fantuzzo. n.d. An integration: Christian maturity and positive mental health. *Journal of Psychology and Christianity* 2:26–38.

Morgan, John H. 1975. Silence as creative therapy. *Journal of Pastoral Care* 29 (December): 248–251.

Morgan, Oliver J. 1987. Pastoral counseling and petitionary prayer. *Journal of Religion and Health* 26 (Summer): 149–152.

Moskal, Brian S. 1990. A time to keep silence. *Industry Week*, 22 January, 27.

Mostrom, Donald G. 1983. *Intimacy with God*. Wheaton: Tyndale.

Murray, Andrew. 1983. *Confession: The road to forgiveness*. Springdale: Whitaker.

Myra, Harold L. 1988. Living by God's surprises. *Leadership* 9 (Fall): 24–30.

Nouwen, Henri J. M. 1972. *With open hands*. Notre Dame: Ave Maria 1981a. *Making all things new*. San Francisco: Harper & Row.1981b. *The way of the heart*. New York: Ballantine.

Oates, Wayne E. 1979. *Nurturing silence in a noisy heart*. Garden City: Doubleday.

Olsen, Lani L. J. 1984. Lessons on the simple life. *One World* 98 (August–September): 19–20.

Ortberg, John C. 1991. One minute maturity. *Leadership* 12 (Spring): 26–31.

Packer, J. I. 1973. *Knowing God*. Downers Grove: InterVarsity.

_____.1990. An introduction to systematic spirituality. *Crux* 26 (March): 2–8.

Palmer, Scott W., ed. 1954.*The confessions of Jacob Boehme*. New York: Harper & Row.

Parker, Percy Livingstone, ed. n.d.*The journal of John Wesley*. Chicago: Moody.

Pascal, Blaise. 1958. *Pascal's pensees*. New York: Dutton.

Pennington, M. Basil. 1982. *Centering prayer*. New York: Image.

Peterson, Eugene H. 1987.*Working the angles: The shape of pastoral integrity*. Grand Rapids: Eerdmans 1988. Growth: An act of the will: *Leadership* 9 (Fall); 34–40.

———. 1989. *The contemplative pastor: Returning to the art of spiritual direction*. Carol Stream: Christianity Today.

———. 1991a. Listen Yahweh. *Christianity Today*, 14 January, 24–25.

———. 1991b. Stumbling across the supernatural. *Leadership* 12 (Summer): 82–90.

Poloma, Margaret M., and Brian F. Pendleton. 1981. Experiences on measures of general well-being. *Journal of Psychology and Theology* 19 (Winter): 71–83.

Progoff, Ira. 1957. *The cloud of unknowing*. New York: Julian.

Rack, Henry. 1969. *Twentieth century spirituality*. London: Epworth.

Radcliffe, Lynn J.1952. *Making prayer real*. New York: Abingdon-Cokesbury.

Ramm, Bernard. 1970. *Protestant biblical interpretation: A textbook of hermeneutics*. Grand Rapids: Eerdmans.

Reid, Clyde. 1974. *Celebrate the temporary*. San Francisco: Harper.

Richards, Lawrence, I. 1987. *A practical theology of spirituality*. Grand Rapids: Zondervan.

Ross-Bryant, Lynn. 1981. *Imagination and the life of the spirit*. Chico: Scholars Press.

Ryken, Leland. 1974. *The literature of the Bible*. Grand Rapids: Zondervan.

Schaeffer, Francis A. 1971. *True spirituality*. Wheaton: Tyndale.

Schleiermacher, Friedrich. 1958. *On religion*. New York: Harper & Row.

Selement, George, and Bruce C. Wooley, eds. 1981. *The confessions of Thomas Shepherd*. Boston: The Society.

Senn, Frank C, ed. 1986. *Protestant spiritual traditions*. New York: Paulist.

Shelley, Bruce. 1988. *All the saints adore thee*. Grand Rapids: Zondervan.

Sider, Ron, ed. 1980. *Living more simply: Biblical principles and practical models*. Downers Grove: InterVarsity.

Simons, George F. 1975. *Journal for life*. 2 vols. Chicago: Life in Christ.

Sine, Tom. 1988. More is less: Add some celebration to your life. *The Other Side* 24 (March): 37.

Smith, Chuck. 1991. What to make of mystic moments. *Leadership* 12 (Summer): 34–39.

Smith, David R. 1969. *Fasting: A neglected discipline*. Fort Washington: Christian Literature Crusade.

Smith, R. Gregor. 1966. *Secular Christianity*. London: Collins.

Steer, Roger. 1987. *Admiring God: The best of George Mueller*. London: Hodder and Stoughton.

Sterrett, Norton T. 1974. *How to understand your Bible*. Downers Grove: InterVarsity.

Stevens, Edward. 1990. *Spiritual technologies: A user's manual*. New York: Paulist.

Stott, John R. 1964. *Confess your sins: The way of reconciliation*. Philadelphia: Westminster.

Stowell, Joseph M.1986. *Fan the flame*. Chicago: Moody.

Sweeting, George. 1985. *You can climb higher*. Nashville: Thomas Nelson.

Taylor, Jeremy. 1988. *Holy living*. Orleans: Paraclete.

Tillich, Paul J. 1957. Let us dare to have solitude. *Quarterly Review* 12 (May): 9–15.

Todd, Elizabeth. 1985. The value of confession and forgiveness according to Jung. *Journal of Religion and Health* 24 (Spring): 39–48.

Tozer, A. W. 1982. *The pursuit of God*. Camp Hill: Christian.

———. 1984. *Keys to the deeper life*. Grand Rapids: Zondervan.

Traina, Robert A. 1952.*Methodical Bible study: A new approach to hermeneutics*. Wilmore: Asbury.

Trueblood, D. Elton. 1936. *The essence of spiritual religion*. San Francisco: Harper.

Underhill, Evelyn. 1926. *Concerning the inner life*. New York: Dutton.

———.1940. *Mysticism: A study in the nature and development of man's spiritual consciousness*. London: Methuen.

———. 1943. *Practical mysticism*. New York: Dutton.

Unger, Merrill F. 1984. *The New Unger's Bible Handbook*. 2d ed. Chicago: Moody.

Vos, Howard F. 1956. *Effective Bible study: A guide to sixteen methods*. Grand Rapids: Eerdmans.

Wakefield,Gordon S.ed. 1983. *The Westminster dictionary of Christian spirituality*. Philadelphia: Westminster. S.v. "Asceticism," by Rosemary Rader.

Wald, Oletta. 1975. *The joy of discovery in Bible study*. Minneapolis: Augsburg.

Wallis, Arthur. 1968. *God's chosen fast*. Fort Washington: Christian Literature Crusade.

Walsh, James, James, ed. n.d. *Spirituality through the centuries: Ascetics and mystics of the western church*. New York: P. J. Kenedy.

Waltke, Bruce K. 1987. Hermeneutics and the spiritual life. *Crux* 1 (March): 5–10.

———. 1988. Evangelical spirituality: A biblical scholar's perspective. *Journal of the Evangelical Theological* Society 31 (March): 9–24.

Webb, William Walter. 1982. *The cure of souls: A manual for the clergy*. New York: James Pott.

Wesley, John. 1836. Causes of the inefficacy of Christianity. In *Sermons on several occasions*. 2 vols. New York: Waugh and Mason. *The journal of John Wesley*. Chicago: Moody.

White, John. 1976. *The fight*. Downers Grove: InterVarsity.

Whitney, Donald S. 1991. *Spiritual disciplines for the Christian life*. Colorado Springs: Navpress.

Whyte, Alexander, n.d. *Lord, teach us to pray*. New York: Harper.

Wiersbe, Warren W. 1976. *Walking with the giants*. Grand Rapids: Baker.

Willard, Dallas. 1988. *The spirit of the disciplines: Understanding how God changes lives*. San Francisco: Harper & Row.

Willimon, William H. 1989. The pointlessness of praise. *Christian Ministry* 20 (May–June): 29–30.

Woolman, John. 1972. *The journal of John Woolman*. Secaucus: Citadel.

Yancey, Phillip. 1984. Learning to live with money. *Christianity Today*, 14 December, 30–42.

Made in the USA
Middletown, DE
27 August 2016